About the Book

"Leo Bottary has done it again—and just in time for the new rules of work. Building on *The Power of Peers*, Bottary's new book, *Peernovation*, takes proven concepts for CEO peer groups to higher levels of team insights and company performance. In a post-COVID world, and with the emergence of AI across even more industries, *Peernovation* reminds us of what *doesn't* change: our humanity and our ability to collaborate and create. These will be the keys to thriving in the decades to come."

Rich Karlgaard, publisher and futurist, *Forbes*

"Outstanding book for CEOs, CFOs, and other senior executives dealing with the transition to agile. Some cool takeaways/reminders about human nature and teamwork. Leo has the rare gift as an author of taking difficult abstract concepts and translating them into an accessible, enjoyable narrative. Highly engaging, entertaining, readable, and full of well-explained big ideas. Read this book and learn from one of the best."

Dr. Amarendra Bhushan Dhiraj, CEO and editorial director, *CEOWORLD* magazine

"Leo Bottary is the ultimate expert regarding how peers add value to an organization. In his latest book, *Peernovation*, he artfully explores the factors that lead to high-performing groups and team effectiveness. In a time when teams must create globally impactful advances, it has never been more critical to learn how to get beyond silos, recognize the value of peers, expand perspective to make better decisions, and learn to work more effectively together."

Dr. Diane Hamilton, author of *Cracking the Curiosity Code*

"Leo has become the voice of inclusion. With an open mind and an open heart, we can become greater together. To innovate forward, to thrive in a novel economy, the idea of Peernovation is paramount, especially in a time of great divide."

Brian Solis, digital anthropologist, best-selling author, keynote speaker

"One role of leaders is to look outside themselves and their companies for new ideas and opportunities. Thriving in times of change is all about the people. We increase our likelihood of success with a strong community of diverse thinking, inspiration, and support. Leo's Peernovation framework shows a way to maximize mutual peer advantage."

Scott Mordell, Former CEO of YPO (formerly
the Young Presidents Organization)

"Teamwork makes the dream work. As the business world slowly enters an era of collaboration and abundance, Leo's work is a guide for leaders to explore the infinite mastermind potential of their teams."

Alexander Keehnen, founder and CEO, W.I.N. Mastermind

An individual is simply no match for a group or team. With *Peernovation*, Leo has hit a home run with the notion that when we have a common purpose and shared values, we work together to make each other better and create something larger than ourselves. Leveraging your best judgment and the perspectives of your trusted peers will help you remain an effective leader. Our purpose of helping high-integrity leaders make great decisions that benefit their companies, families, and communities has never been more important."

Sam Reese, CEO of Vistage Worldwide

"In *Peernovation*, Leo will show you how to surround yourself with a strategic group of peers and then harness those relationships to dramatically improve your thinking, your decision-making, your teamwork, and your ability to make a difference in the world."

Craig Weber, author of *Conversational Capacity* and *Influence in Action*

"Leo Bottary gives us the playbook we need to embrace and embody this truth. He helps us get from Me to We and shows us through creative anecdotes, thoughtful exercises, and the research to back it up that when there is teamwork and collaboration, wonderful things can be achieved."

Angela Maiers, founder, Choose2Matter

"Me to We is the path to success personally, for companies, and in society. In this excellent read, Leo connects the dots between peer groups and work teams, and he shows us the path forward in our evolution as humans."

Dan Hoffman, CEO and founder, Circles

"The adaptation of the ladder of inference into the reflexive loop is a marvelous tool and captures the true essence of beliefs and behaviors and the connection between them required in leadership. Leo Bottary has been an inspiration to the world of peer advisory and understands the importance of being part of this model for true team success. He takes the concept to a new level in what he calls Peernovation, which will ultimately bring a clearer understanding of how the power of groups wins every time in the pursuit of perspective on complex and important decisions. Thank you, Leo, for sharing your guidance and inspiration to the leaders of industry."

Todd Millar, president and CEO, and TEC Executive Chair at TEC Canada

"There are two types of leaders, in general: those who have to be the smartest in the room and those who surround themselves with really talented teams. If you are in the category of the smartest in the room, this book is not for you. If you want to learn how to attract, empower, and coalesce a high-performing team, congratulations; you have found the ideal book to achieve team nirvana."

Katina Koller, Vistage chair and EOS implementer

"*The Power of Peers* was the seed that inspired us to invite Leo to come to our hometown [Porto, Portugal] four years ago. He joined Ryan Foland and Rahfeal Gordon to speak to entrepreneurs about how mastermind groups could help them scale. During the visit, we all formed our own peer group that began in earnest during a 14k run through the streets of Porto and still continues today. *Peernovation* is a terrific read that demonstrates Leo's commitment to building better leaders, stronger teams, and a more collaborative world. We are grateful for his friendship and for having read his third and best book yet."

Mike Dias and Mary Menezes, Co-CEOs, ScaleUpValley.com

Peernovation is *the* book you need to help navigate through the massive paradigm shift every business owner is currently facing. Our ability to interpret data, make critical decisions, and navigate the challenge of business cannot be done alone. Your peers face the same challenges as you. Together we are stronger."

Ronan Leonard, founder, Eccountability Virtual Masterminds

If you want a high-performing team (and who wouldn't?), then Leo Bottary's new book, *Peernovation*, will give you all you need to know. He teaches us that we learn better when we learn together with our peers because of a reinforcing and repeating loop of learning, sharing, applying, and achieving. He proves this over and over again with case studies that illustrate the five factors common to high-performing groups. The term Peernovation unites peers with innovation, and Leo shows us how to do that. What more could you want?"

Deborah Spring Laurel, cofounder, the Peer Learning Institute

"A must read for twenty-first-century leaders, Peernovation is one of the most important principles of our time. Being challenged to think differently is what drives success and economic growth, and Leo Bottary nails it in this engaging and practical guide to maximizing potential in the most challenging environment we have experienced in generations."

Laura Gordon, chair, Vistage UK

"In a world of rapid change, engaging with and learning from others is essential for success. In *Peernovation*, Leo Bottary provides facts, examples, and actions everyone can take to use the principles of peer collaboration to build, participate, and lead high-performance teams. A great read for anyone."

Jennifer Vessels, founder, Executive Growth Alliance and CEO, Next Step

"Leo has done it again, truly at the forefront of peer observation and the undeniable power of the peers. His first book enabled us to understand the literal power. This book allows us to understand, on a far deeper level, the amazing things that can be achieved when you collaborate and innovate. So much can be learned and then implemented for our teams and organizations to ensure that we succeed and advance forward. The possibilities are endless. We just need permission and the framework, and Leo covers both."

Adam Harris, Helping People Create and Have Presence

"In *Peernovation*, Leo has added the depth of experiences, stories, and a framework for continuous learning, for yourself as a leader, your peers, and the people you lead. Paraphrased from *Peernovation*, ' If we are to thrive in the future together ... then we need to expand our circle of friends and colleagues, listen for understanding, demand better from our media, expect more from our leaders, and build on what we can agree upon.' The journey to become a better you crystallizes the insights from *Peernovation*.

Cecelia K. Houser, Ed.D., principal, Korn Ferry

"In watching Leo Bottary work for the last decade or so, I've noticed a consistent message that he touts: The collective group is always significantly better than the individual. Never has that been clearer than in his latest book, *Peernovation*. Having been part of some of the high-performing CEO peer groups he's studied—both as a member and as a speaker—it's evident he has worked with some of the best leaders of people to provide you with a framework, a framework that will help you guide your team, so you never again see someone's shoulders shrug or hear them utter the words, 'That's just the way we've always done it.' If you follow his advice and choose your own adventure within the framework, your team will be innovative, creative, and effective. Read the book, study it, implement it, and then read it again."

Gini Dietrich, founder and author, *Spin Sucks*

"As an entrepreneur and CEO, I've relied heavily on three resources to be successful: a network of generous peers, talented and dedicated teams, and books like *Peernovation* that keep me and my work at the forefront of what's next. So, as you can imagine, any book that can show me how to leverage my peers more effectively and inspire my teams to perform even better is a must-read. I highly recommend it to any team leader or member."

André Eidskrem, founder, IntraHouse

"In a business world where the main focus is the state of our P&Ls, Leo Bottary challenges us with the notion that organizations can be more innovative, impactful, and profitable if we start asking, 'How can we help our teams be happier and more productive?' In *Peernovation*, Leo shares his journey from me to we, using his proven work with peer groups to help us turn our attention to what makes a strong P&L possible: high-performing teams. If you want to thrive in the years ahead, add *Peernovation* to your reading list."

Jay Izso, CEO, Coaching Mavericks

"I have learned the hard way that who you surround yourself with matters. Leo's book, *Peernovation*, outlines a framework to harness the power of peer influence. The pages are filled with practical advice that shows why being more selective, strategic, and structured about the people we choose to surround ourselves with, is ultimately the driving force behind our success."

Ryan Foland, speaker and author of *Ditch the Act: Reveal the Surprising Power of the Real You for Greater Success.*

"For over twenty-five years, I have experienced the power of bringing people together with different backgrounds, experiences, industries, and stages of business life cycles. When groups 'work together to make each other better' and get to transformational levels, they are considered 'high-performing.' Check. But the possibility to 'create something larger than themselves' for the group and their respective teams': Challenge on."

Janet Fogarty, master chair, *Vistage Worldwide*

Peernovation is the next step in Leo Bottary's journey that starts with how high-performing teams function and leads us to a place where a carefully selected group makes each other better and creates something larger than themselves. I enjoyed reading Leo's latest book and uncovering the way he marries the concepts of a peer (people like me) with innovation (creativity realized). I, too, believe in the power of collective intelligence, and Leo does an outstanding job explaining how we must be intentional in leveraging peer influence and peer advantage to our mutual benefit."

Richard Franzi, visionary, Critical Mass for Business

"If there is one definite book you need to read about cultivating and strategically establishing an effective group for great results, it would be *Peernovation*. Never has a book like this come at a more perfect time in our current society. This book highlights profound knowledge for excellent teamwork. Leo does a flawless job in articulating some of the best methods and insights to help all of us elevate our group of peers. Great job, Leo."

Rahfeal Gordon, CEO, Madison + Park Global Branding Agency

"Learning what's in this book is valuable for your career whether you're just starting out, nearing the top or anywhere in between."

May (Chien) Busch, *Executive Coach, Speaker, Advisor, Author*

"Since harnessing *The Power of Peers* in his first book and illustrating *What Anyone Can Do* by surrounding yourself with the right people in his second book, Leo shines a light on a new aspect of peer influence with *Peernovation*. Leo dives into how shared values and common purpose from who you surround yourself with can lead to bigger and better outcomes than ever imagined. Consider *Peernovation* the next step in your journey to tap into the superpower of your peers."

George Glover, *chair, Vistage Worldwide*

"*Peernovation* is a must-read book for anyone who wants to achieve greatness in all that they do by leveraging the power that an effectively managed and led team can bring. The framework that Leo shares, which is based on more than a decade of academic and experiential research, will revolutionize the way your team operates. Apply his wisdom today and you will enjoy the benefits that it will bring."

Simon Alexander Ong, Executive Coach and International Speaker

PEER NOVATION

What Peer Advisory Groups Can Teach Us about Building High-Performing Teams

LEO BOTTARY

Copyright © 2020 Leo Bottary.

All rights reserved. No part of this book may be used or reproduced by any means, graphic, electronic, or mechanical, including photocopying, recording, taping or by any information storage retrieval system without the written permission of the author except in the case of brief quotations embodied in critical articles and reviews.

This book is a work of non-fiction. Unless otherwise noted, the author and the publisher make no explicit guarantees as to the accuracy of the information contained in this book and in some cases, names of people and places have been altered to protect their privacy.

Archway Publishing books may be ordered through booksellers or by contacting:

Archway Publishing
1663 Liberty Drive
Bloomington, IN 47403
www.archwaypublishing.com
844-669-3957

Because of the dynamic nature of the Internet, any web addresses or links contained in this book may have changed since publication and may no longer be valid. The views expressed in this work are solely those of the author and do not necessarily reflect the views of the publisher, and the publisher hereby disclaims any responsibility for them.

Any people depicted in stock imagery provided by Getty Images are models, and such images are being used for illustrative purposes only. Certain stock imagery © Getty Images.

Interior Image Credit: Emily Christensen, Paper Cake Creative

ISBN: 978-1-4808-9566-9 (sc)
ISBN: 978-1-4808-9568-3 (hc)
ISBN: 978-1-4808-9567-6 (e)

Library of Congress Control Number: 2020917137

Print information available on the last page.

Archway Publishing rev. date: 10/14/2020

To my wife, Diane, and the most amazing family I could ever ask for.

Individually, we are one drop. Together, we are an ocean.[1]
—Ryunosuke Satoro

CONTENTS

Foreword xvii
Preface xix
Introduction: A Shift in Mindset xxi

Chapter 1	What Peernovation Looks Like	1
Chapter 2	The Right People	19
Chapter 3	Psychological Safety	31
Chapter 4	Productivity	43
Chapter 5	Accountability	55
Chapter 6	Leadership	69
Chapter 7	Common Challenges and How to Meet Them ...	81
Chapter 8	What Peernovation Means for Teams and the Journey from Me to We	95

Afterword 109
Acknowledgments 113
About the Author 115
Notes 117
References 121

FOREWORD

For years, even decades, we have been conditioned to follow certain rules, certain guidelines, and certain behaviors. "It's how we do things around here" was how it was normally phrased. Once upon a time, that was what got you ahead. Keep your head down, do your job, and live happily ever after. Who made up those rules, anyway? Where is it written that we all have to stick to a homogeneous routine? It may have worked in the past, but in the everchanging world of business, that doesn't get you anywhere.

I understand the comfort found in a routine. It sometimes brings order to the chaos that seems to constantly be around us, a sense of grounding even. Routine makes us comfortable, but it doesn't make us grow. In order to do that, we have to push past our comfort zones; we have to push boundaries and get out of the silos that we've been grouped into, by chance or by choice.

We have to fight the urge to remain safe in our own silos and burst onto the scene like we own the joint. We have to expand our horizons, which in turn gives us a wider perspective and allows us to be better decision-makers. When we are capable of seeing multiple possibilities, we see and experience different perspectives, and the decisions we make are based on rationale, not emotion. It's like our very own Enlightenment Age, of sorts.

Once we open our minds to myriad possibilities, perspectives, and ways of thinking, we abandon the "me" mentality and fall into the "we" mentality. If you've ever played any sports, that concept has been drilled into your brain more than anything else. You win as a team; you lose as a team. That's how teamwork works. But in order for the team to win, everyone has to play their position and play it well. Your starters are your A players. They're your workhorses, those who stay late after practice and those who come in early. Sure, there's always someone who scores more points and gets most of the glory, but those players can't score if they don't have the ball. It requires someone to provide the assist in order to put some points on the board.

As leaders, we have to make it very clear to our team the position they're playing. Certain players will take the glory some days, while others will get their turn in the spotlight later on. Whoever gets the glory becomes irrelevant once they understand the concept of teamwork. There's no "I" in team, and that mentality needs to permeate throughout the organization; everyone needs to be using the same playbook. That's how you learn, that's how you grow, and that's how you push boundaries: together.

Leo's book delivers clear-cut examples of what can be achieved when everyone is rowing in the same direction, not because they all agree all the time, but because everyone excels at playing their position, have learned from one another, and can play as a cohesive unit.

Jeffrey Hayzlett, Primetime TV and Podcast Host, Speaker, Author, and Part-Time Cowboy

PREFACE

Peernovation is about the significance of working together for something larger than ourselves. As it turns out, nearly half the book was written or finalized during a period of shelter in place amid the 2020 pandemic. The phrase "who you surround yourself with matters" has never been more relevant, so avoiding a reference to the global health situation as part of this narrative wasn't an option. In these times, we've discovered that social distancing is every bit an act of caring as a loving embrace, a tacit recognition that we're all in this together, and that as one, we will do whatever it takes to weather this storm (and whatever else comes our way).

While keeping our distance, we are touching one another in profound ways. We revere the courage of health care workers who, at great personal risk, are treating coronavirus patients and helping them return safely to their families. We agonize with them because they can't save everyone, and we weep for them when they themselves become victims. Our hearts go out to seniors, who as a highly at-risk population during this pandemic have become increasingly isolated from society. We marvel at local restaurants and other small businesses and offer as much support as we can. As these businesses face their own struggles, they find ways to continue to serve their communities, whether it's providing free meals to those in need or pivoting their operations to produce masks or other personal protective equipment for those on the front lines.

While enjoying a newly energized love of family, working from home with screaming kids and barking dogs can take its toll on our cognitive and emotional stability. Yet when we need a mental break, we check out our favorite media resource, where human creativity abounds. It's where we find our fellow citizens of the world singing from balconies to their neighbors, joining drive-by celebrations for a child's birthday, or creating obstacle courses for their bored kids and stir-crazy parents. We participate in virtual happy hours with our friends, families, and coworkers, all while discovering new ways to work and play during these trying times.

We mourn those who died and grieve with those who lost loved ones. When all of this is over (a new reality, notwithstanding), it will be up to us to reflect on this collective experience and remember what really matters. Going forward, let's be kind to everyone we meet, seek to learn rather than judge, and focus on what truly gives our life meaning: each other. Together, with love and kindness in our hearts, anything is possible.

INTRODUCTION: A SHIFT IN MINDSET

None of us is as smart as all of us.[2]
—Kenneth H. Blanchard

We see life in siloes, in part because that's how we were raised. Most of us grew up in families and neighborhoods that provided an understandably narrow view of the world. We went to schools that offered separate classes for each subject, with minimal overlap from one to the other. To put this in context, I was born in 1959 and attended public school in the 1960s and '70s. I'm not sure how it worked at your school, but when I was taught history, for example, it was in the form of dates, generals, kings and queens, global expeditions, battles, and the ever-evolving shift of power. We may have learned what was happening in a specific country from a political and military perspective, but we gained little understanding of how the people lived, what was really going on, and why.

Attending separate classes for English, math, science, art, music, based on curriculum guidelines for each subject, was orderly and neat, but it robbed us in so many ways. Imagine for a moment if your education had been seamlessly coordinated, so that as you were studying a particular era in history, your English class was covering the prevailing literature of the time. In other classes, while one teacher was painting a picture of how art reflected a country's way of life, another was having you listen to music and providing insights about it that connected with your broader understanding of the times. The reinforcing nature of such an approach would not only have been more engaging but also more educational and memorable.

If you work in a company today, you're probably part of a department: marketing, finance, human resources, sales, operations, and so on. Not unlike the example offered from my educational experience growing up, the more we stay in our respective department (or silo), the less likely we are to understand what's really happening in our company or industry and determine how we can make a positive contribution to it.

The Lingering Impact of a Limited Perspective

It's challenging enough that from childhood, we're structurally placed in situations that limit our perspective, but the research is clear when it comes to its lingering impact. I've often wondered how two people can witness the same event and have diametrically opposing views about what happened. Among my favorite experiences from graduate school was learning about Chris Argyris's Ladder of Inference.[3] As you consider this ladder, examine figure 1 and look closely at the reinforcing progression of what we observe, how we add meaning, make assumptions, draw conclusions, and adopt beliefs that shape the way we see the world.

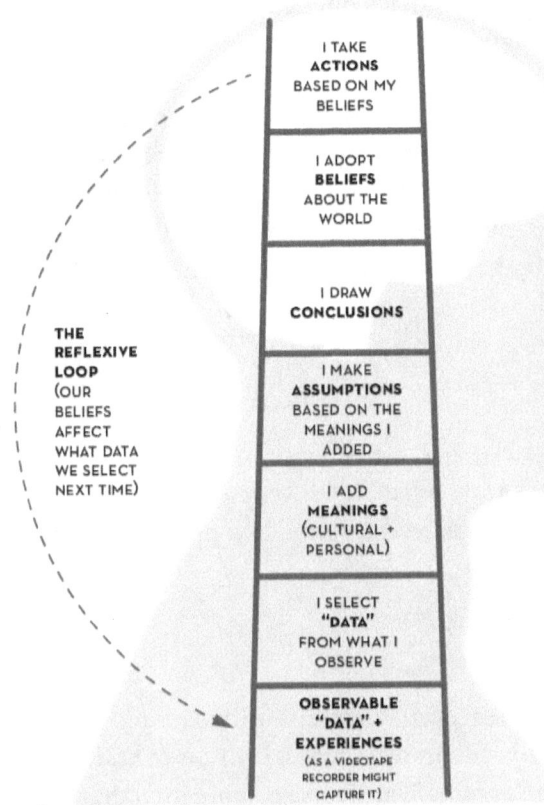

Figure 1. Ladder of Inference

Think about someone you know and try walking up the ladder. To offer an example, I'll pick a politician as part of a nonpartisan exercise to demonstrate how the concept works and to illustrate its cyclical nature. Whether I select Barack Obama or Donald Trump, both offer equally excellent examples of public figures who some people love and others despise. Party and political views come into play, but there's much more going on here.

Let's look at how two voters (Howard and Christine) may have perceived Barack Obama during his first campaign for president:

I observe the available data: young, contemplative, Harvard educated, African American, former constitutional law professor, excellent speaker, community organizer, and so on. Assume the list continues with hundreds of other data points across a broad spectrum.

I select data: Of course, different people will choose entirely different sets of data based on the beliefs they've adopted about what's important (which you'll find further up the ladder, hence the cycle). But even if two people select the same data points, they can still reach very different conclusions. For this exercise, let's choose young, contemplative, and Harvard educated.

I add meaning:

Howard: inexperienced, indecisive, arrogant
Christine: energetic, thoughtful, intelligent
(Other people would look at the same data points and add their own meanings).

I make assumptions:

Howard: His inexperience will hurt him with regard to getting anything done in Washington; his indecisiveness will be considered a personal weakness, and there's arguably no worse combination than someone who is arrogant and inexperienced.

Christine: His lack of Washington experience may be his biggest strength; his thoughtful approach will make both sides of the aisle feel they are being heard and included, and his intelligence is essential to leading in this complex world.

I draw conclusions:

Howard: He'll be a terrible president.
Christine: He's just what our country needs.

I adopt beliefs:

Howard: A young, contemplative Harvard-educated guy may make a great professor, but he'll be an ineffective commander-in-chief.

Christine: A young, contemplative Harvard-educated guy offers the energy and qualities necessary to lead our nation.

I act:

Howard voted against Obama (and even campaigned for his opponent). Christine voted for Obama (sent a donation or volunteered).

The key is to examine our beliefs, explore where they come from, consider the role they play in shaping how we see the world (the data we select), and understand how others can look at the very same person or situation and reach vastly different conclusions. This can be especially challenging when we tend to watch polarizing news programming that aligns with our current worldview.

The phenomenon here is popularly referred to as the Echo Chamber: "an environment where a person only encounters information or opinions that reflect and reinforce their own. Echo chambers can create misinformation and distort a person's perspective, so they have difficulty considering opposing viewpoints and discussing complicated topics. They're fueled in part by confirmation bias, which is the tendency to favor info that reinforces existing beliefs."[4]

Echo Chamber: "an environment where a person only encounters information or opinions that reflect and reinforce their own.

Here is an open letter I wrote to the Cable News Networks:

> Dear Cable News:
>
> In recent weeks, I've had the good fortune to spend time with some hard-working public servants on both sides

of the aisle on Capitol Hill. I also just returned from the Milken Institute's Global Conference in Los Angeles, where thought leaders from around the world talked about the difficult challenges facing America. The good news is that there are many, many smart people out there who believe that while some of the problems our nation faces are difficult to say the least, they ARE solvable. The bad news is that the political climate has become so toxic that good people who care deeply about this country, but who have honest intellectual differences about how to solve our nation's problems, risk personal and political vilification every time they try to reach across the aisle or share an idea that actually might make sense.

We have an untenable environment for honest problem solving, and, quite frankly, cable news is doing nothing but making it worse (and the networks/other news outlets aren't much better). You share meaningless polling data, give airtime to whoever is willing to be the most outrageous, and provide a platform for attacking people rather than challenging their ideas. You're serving a 24/7 multiple-course meal of political red meat, which you've "super-sized" in recent years, and not surprisingly, we're feeling the impact on our nation's health. You've been a willing accomplice to drawing political lines in the sand that have made it all but impossible for serious people to agree on sensible solutions for the country. Worse yet, you discourage good people from entering into public service at a time when we need all the good people we can get!

It's a bit like the boiling frog syndrome. Put a frog in water, turn up the heat gradually, and the frog will eventually boil alive. I suggest it's time to turn down the heat, or this country risks suffering the same fate. I know it's not sexy. I realize that more people watch Fox News than C-SPAN, but our country faces serious problems, and you can actually make a positive contribution to the dialogue. We need a media which seeks to inform rather than frighten and anger. I believe your viewers and your sponsors would appreciate it, and even more importantly, you could give our leaders a chance to do the serious work they were elected to do.

I want to thank the hard-working staffers and elected officials in Washington, the amazing people I met at the Milken Institute Global Conference, and the numerous small business leaders out there for everything they do to make our country better. They've inspired me to draft this short post, which by itself may be meaningless, but if others agree with me, then maybe they'll write to you as well. I hope they do, and I hope you pay attention.

Thank you.[5]

It saddens me to say that this letter was written in May 2011. Unfortunately, the situation has only worsened. Given this environment and because most of us don't sit around and constantly re-examine our beliefs, it perpetuates a continual cycle that over time makes us even less open to new perspectives. If we are to thrive in the future together, which is the only way we're going to do it, then we need to break this cycle. We can do so by expanding our circle of friends and colleagues, listening for understanding, demanding better from our media, expecting more from our leaders, and building on what we can agree upon.

INDIVIDUALS VERSUS GROUPS AND TEAMS

When I speak to large audiences, I often begin with a brief exercise that dramatically illustrates the difference between the efforts of an individual and what we are capable of doing as a group or team. I invite an audience member (let's call her Sarah) to pretend she is attending a championship game that involves her favorite sports team. At the count of three, I ask Sarah to cheer, clap, or yell, as if she were experiencing the moment her team wins the title. (Doing this alone in front of a large crowd makes most people feel a bit self-conscious, to say the least.) Sarah generously plays along, but of course, no matter how hard she tries, filling a large room with sound with a single voice is no easy task.

Then I ask everyone to join Sarah in the exercise. At the count of three, as you might imagine, the collective effort blows the roof off the place, and not one person feels self-conscious about their participation. They achieved an exponentially more dramatic result and were far more comfortable doing so. Why? Because they did it together. If I challenged them to do it again, they would have created a louder, even more joyous sound.

My Road from Me to We

In 2006, I returned to school for my Master of Arts in Strategic Communication and Leadership (MASCL) at Seton Hall University. It had been a while since receiving my BA in 1983, and let's just say the student experience was quite a bit different from what I had remembered. I soon discovered that getting my master's was not a solo pursuit. I wasn't there just to listen to my professors, read books/journal articles, write papers, and take exams. I was part of a cohort now, where collaborating with my fellow students was core to the learning model. Having spent the bulk of my time as a student during the late 1960s through the early '80s, this was a foreign concept to me. I often joked that back when I was in school, collaborating was called "cheating."

> *An individual is simply no match for a group or team.*

In this case, we were mid-to-senior level executives, all with rich experiences, hailing from different parts of the country. We brought our own knowledge that came from years of working at a range of organizations in our respective fields. Our professors recognized the intellectual capital in the room, and they taught us how to access it, all while we learned from them and the material they assigned. If you ask anyone from that program, they will tell you we learned as much from one another as we did from the faculty and the assigned material. To be clear, our professors would not regard that as a diss; they would be delighted by it. It was exactly what they were trying to achieve from the moment we first met at orientation residency to graduation (and through the learning journey we continue to enjoy today).

I grew to love my cohort and to this day regard it among the best collective experiences I've ever had. That said, I wasn't always the best cohort member. My journey from "me to we," or from old school to new school, was fraught with times when I unfairly judged the commitment, effort, and perspectives of others. I even called out fellow students publicly and, on occasion, behaved in a way that was not particularly constructive. Fortunately, my fellow students and professors were there to help me become a better teammate.

When I started MASCL, earning a 4.0 was the last thing on my mind. And without the help of my cohort, it never would have happened. My study partner, Dean Acosta, who also received a 4.0, would tell you the same thing in assessing his own performance. Dean and I forged a bond from the very first day, after both of us were scolded for arriving late to the orientation. As I reflect on my time in the program, doing my part to help others realize their potential is something I regard as the most rewarding part of the experience. The truth is, none of us did it alone.

Having served students as an adjunct professor for more than twelve years now (at Seton Hall, Northeastern, and Rutgers), I do my best to pay it forward. I want them to see their fellow students for their gifts (not judge their faults), appreciate different perspectives, work together productively, and achieve outcomes more significant than any individual ever could. The very best students I teach today don't merely perform well as individuals; they actively contribute to making everyone around them better. It's a beautiful thing, and it's as important in business as it is in school.

WHAT GREAT GROUPS DO

When Leon Shapiro and I conducted the research for our book, *The Power of Peers: How the Company You Keep Drives Leadership, Growth & Success*, the premise was to explore why formal

> **We learn better when we learn together.**

peer groups for CEOs and business leaders are so effective. We thought if we could crack the code and give language to the peer advisory group category, we would inspire more leaders to join a group of their own. Our research involved examining the academic literature, collecting documents from organizations that ran business-related peer groups, interviewing members and leaders of those groups, talking to people who started their own peer groups, and keeping our eyes and ears open as we sat in on group meetings in the United States and around the world.

We defined a high-performing peer group as one that had a robust learning-achieving cycle.

Figure 2. Learning-Achieving Cycle

The learning-achieving cycle is a reinforcing loop of learning, sharing, applying, achieving, learning, sharing, and so on.[6] We learn better when we learn together. Anecdotally, my MASCL learning team members will back me up on this. It's what made our cohort so amazing. If you want some additional data, consider this: When we study alone, we typically remember 28 percent of what we read after two days. After reviewing the material a second time, our retention jumps to 46 percent. Yet when we engage others by asking questions and sharing experiences, we remember 69 percent. The act of learning together creates "memory pathways" that stick in our minds.[7]

Book clubs are a great example of this brand of learning. Bring six people together, have them read the same book, and invite them to talk for a few hours about what they read. Everyone will come away with a deeper understanding of the content that will stick with them longer. High-performing peer groups, however, are about more than just learning for the sake of knowledge acquisition. Great groups engage in productive dialogue that inspires the trial of new ideas in the real world. Great teams do the same thing. It's how the best teams continuously improve.

WHAT'S THE BEST TEAM YOU'VE EVER BEEN PART OF?

In my workshops with mastermind groups, I ask the members this question: "What's the best team you've ever been part of and why?"

I've posed this query to more than 150 groups in North America and the UK. It's a question I'd like you to think about. Consider it in terms of identifying the team itself, and as precisely as you can, make a list of what made your team so special.

> **Great groups engage in productive dialogue that inspires the trial of new ideas in the real world. Great teams do the same thing.**

You might be surprised to learn how many group members say their Little League, Pop Warner, or high school basketball teams when asked this question. Consider for a moment that most of these adults are between thirty-five and sixty-five. It makes me think of two things: 1) That the team experience they had, even though it was so long ago, had such an impact on them that to this day, they can wax poetic about it as if it were yesterday; and 2) How unfortunate it is that they had to go back to Little League baseball to pull an example, that somewhere along the line, they hadn't played on a team or worked for a team worthy of such recognition. What's more, many business leaders can't think of a team at all.

That said, whether it's their Little League team or the team they are part of today, the same attributes tend to emerge. They describe these teams as having people committed to a common purpose, who trusted one another, contributed in different ways, enjoyed a high level of peer-to-peer accountability, and had excellent leadership/coaching. You don't have to hear this explanation too many times to see the obvious comparison between what we learned about high-performing peer groups while writing *The Power of Peers* and the top-performing teams CEOs and business executives described in response to my question.

Why Accessing Multiple Perspectives Matters

As I've been leading more webinars and group sessions via Zoom, I've added a new exercise that illustrates the advantage of accessing multiple perspectives. I show a picture of a large, beautifully furnished room and ask the participants to take a few moments to look at it. After blocking the image from the screen, I call upon individuals to tell us all what they noticed about the room. Suffice it to say that no one individual will capture everything in the room. Because people's eyes tend to be drawn to different objects or features (data points they select on their walk up the ladder of inference), it takes several people to provide a complete picture. Based on individual biases, their responses involve talking about what they see and giving these observations meaning by describing the room's myriad functional possibilities.

I use the term *biases* purposely and not in a pejorative way. Biases are a fact of life. We all have them. Owning up to them and being open to new ideas is how we learn. Imagine the benefit of having an extra-wide ladder of inference. Building that ladder and climbing it together will not only give your group or team greater clarity about what they're seeing, but also offer them a more holistic perspective about what it all means.

Key Terms

In short, we're all in the same boat. We have an enormous impact on one another and, as a result, have an infinite capacity to make each other better. You'll find the following terms key to embracing the ideas in this book.

Groups convene to help their members achieve their individual goals. Many of the groups covered in this book are CEO or key executive groups. In the text, you'll notice that the terms peer groups, peer advisory groups, and mastermind groups are used interchangeably.

Teams work together toward achieving a collective goal or creating a shared work product. Such teams may involve a business team working to develop an innovative product or a sports team seeking to win a championship.

Peer influence speaks to understanding the impact the people who surround us can have in shaping our behavior. It's a formidable force in our lives, one that you've experienced for as long as you can remember.

Peer advantage serves to harness the power of peer influence when we are more selective, strategic, and structured about the people we choose to surround ourselves with. Peer advantage is the driving force behind high-performing groups and teams.

Systems thinking involves identifying patterns of behavior over time and surfacing the underlying structures that drive those patterns. By understanding and changing structures that are not serving us well (including our mental models and ladders of inference), we can expand the available choices and create more effective, long-term solutions to persistent challenges.[8]

Peernovation occurs when a carefully selected group of people, who with a common purpose and shared values, work together to make each other better and create something larger than themselves. Simply put: Peer Advantage + Systems Thinking = *Peernovation*.

PEERNOVATION AND WHY WE SHOULD CARE ABOUT IT

If, by definition, we grow up with a limited perspective that is perpetuated by our ladder of inference and exacerbated by the world we live in, then it seems worthwhile to do what we can to actively expand our perspective to help us make better decisions. If you believe there is strength in numbers, that a great group or team is capable of achieving what no individual can do alone, and that meeting the challenges of the future will require realizing a new level of excellence in our organizations, then *Peernovation* is worth a read. Peer influence, peer advantage, and Peernovation already exist as major forces in our lives. It's up to us to harness them for good.

How This Book Is Organized

Chapter 1 offers an overview of systems thinking, Peernovation, and the five factors common to high-performing groups, including what they mean for teams and how they've evolved since first being introduced in *The Power of Peers*. Because the five factors serve as a framework rather than a prescription, they can be applied to your specific team according to your values, priorities, and goals. Chapters 2–6 take a deep dive into each of the five factors, exploring what they mean and how they can be applied, whether you collaborate virtually or at a single location. The stories and data points provided in these chapters are based on live interaction and pressure testing of the material in workshops with more than 150 CEO/key executive peer groups and cross-functional work teams. Because of the confidential nature of these meetings, I provide real-world examples, but I don't identify the location of the group, the individuals involved, or any details that would compromise confidentiality.

Chapter 7 describes the workshop in greater detail, along with its aggregate findings and most commonly referenced challenges and action steps as they pertain to each of the five factors. Chapter 8 connects what these findings mean for teams. It also offers a closing argument designed to inspire you to use the five-factor framework to take your A players and help them become an A team capable of realizing Peernovation and driving sustainable growth.

Join me on the journey from Me to We. Consider how the five factors could work for you and discover how you can bring Peernovation to your team and your own life. The power of we starts with you.

CHAPTER 1
What Peernovation Looks Like

Alone we can do so little; together we can do so much.[9]
—Helen Keller

ONE OF MY ALL-TIME FAVORITE MOVIES IS *APOLLO 13*, STARRING Tom Hanks. Hanks portrayed astronaut Jim Lovell, and Ed Harris played the part of Gene Kranz, NASA's flight director. I especially enjoyed how the movie started. The Lovells were having a big party at their home. After everyone left, Lovell and his wife looked at the incredible mess that was left behind and joked about selling the house versus cleaning it up. It appeared to be a better option, as all they wanted to do was blink and have the mess go away. That's a feeling many of us experience at one point or another in our lives, but it's certainly not the real reason I loved the movie nor why I'm referencing it here. In addition to its compelling true story, there was a story within the story that serves as a perfect illustration of Peernovation.

If you recall, Apollo 13 was to be the nation's third crewed moon landing—a mission that, believe it or not, was already considered routine, which was among the reasons the television networks balked at providing the live coverage afforded to previous expeditions. That said, two days into the mission, with Apollo 13 approximately 205,000 miles from Earth, the astronauts heard a loud bang, accompanied by fluctuations in electrical power and automatic firing of the attitude control thrusters. It was at this point that Lovell uttered the words, "Houston, we have a problem."[10]

Caution and warning lights showed multiple system failures. The most troubling finding wasn't visible on the instrument panel but out the window of the command module (CM), where Lovell saw oxygen escaping from the rear end of the spacecraft. It was clear to everyone at this point that going to the moon would give way to saving the lives of the three crew members on board.

After the explosion crippled the CM, the three astronauts moved to the lunar module (LM) for much of their flight home. However, the LM wasn't designed to support three astronauts, since only two crew members would have used it to descend to the lunar surface. As a result, rising CO_2 levels compromised the crew's survival. The carbon dioxide scrubbers in the CM were different shapes and sizes from the ones in the LM; they were not interchangeable. The command module used cubic scrubbers, while the lunar module used cylindrical ones. Simply put, the survival of the crew would rest on finding a way to put a square peg in a round hole.

> **the survival of the crew would rest on finding a way to put a square peg in a round hole.**

NASA's engineers in Houston had to solve the problem using only the equipment available to the astronauts on board. Ed Smylie, who was chief of the crew systems division, got his team together, and they came up with the idea to join the CM canisters to the LM's cylindrical canister-sockets by drawing air through a space suit hose.[11]

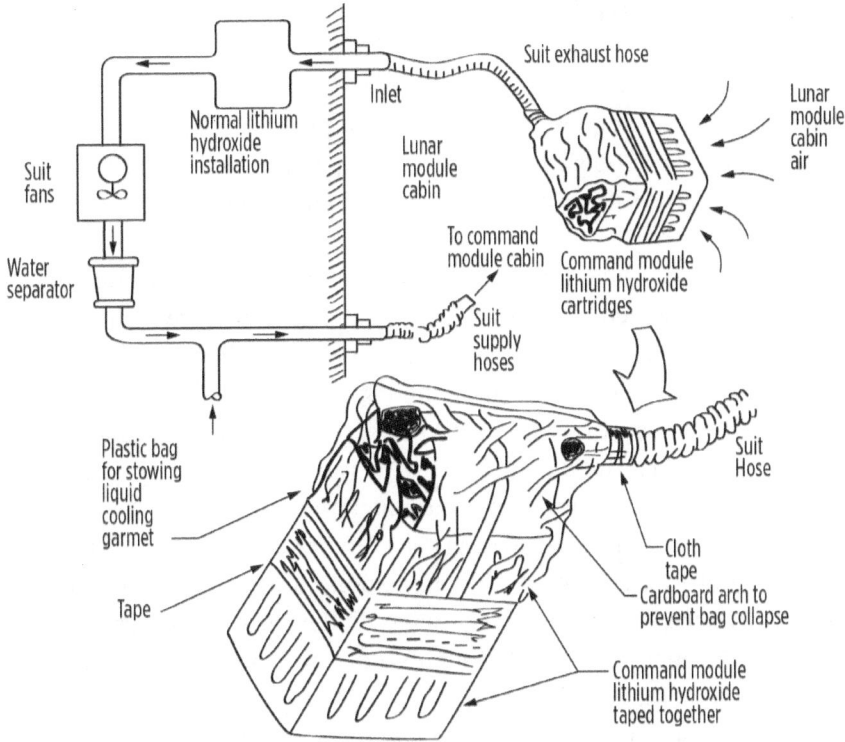

Figure 3. Supplemental CO_2 Removal System, adapted from Apollo 13 Mission Report

Devising a solution to reducing the elevated CO_2 levels was just part of the challenge. Further complicating the matter, Mission Control in Houston couldn't send pictures to the Apollo 13 crew. They had to describe everything verbally. Think of teaching someone how to tie their shoe over the phone and then add several layers of complexity and urgency. As we all know, the workaround was successful, yet it was just one of the many obstacles that team NASA overcame to bring the crew home safely.

CONNECTING THE DOTS

In Steve Jobs's 2005 commencement address at Stanford, he talked about connecting the dots going backward, based on the concept that we don't always understand how what we are learning and experiencing today will be relevant in the future. It's only when we look back that we can connect the dots.[12]

I remember being blown away by the Apollo 13 innovation story, which I first learned about by watching the 1995 feature film. It stuck with me, without ever realizing why. If the sheer impact of the story wasn't enough, a short time after the movie was released in theaters, I happened to cross paths with Apollo 13 flight director Gene Kranz (who thought Ed Harris did a great job, by the way[13]). As you might imagine, this made my initial impression that much more indelible.

Later, there was my learning team experience at Seton Hall, my brief time at Mullen (which I'll share soon), and the position I would eventually accept at Vistage Worldwide in May 2010. In retrospect, they are all very much connected. For those of you who may be unfamiliar with Vistage, it's an organization that facilitates peer advisory groups for CEOs and other business leaders in twenty countries.

Vistage groups typically consist of twelve to sixteen peers from noncompeting businesses and different industries. The members meet once a month in a confidential setting to share the common challenges they face as leaders in their respective organizations. They are committed to helping one another learn and grow, and by all accounts, the groups are extremely effective. When I started at Vistage, I remember people telling me that the whole Vistage concept was challenging to understand. Personally, after having been part of a learning team at Seton Hall, I didn't find it difficult to grasp at all. Seton Hall prepared me to understand Vistage on an accelerated track, without my ever realizing that that's what it was preparing me to do.

> **If the learning-achieving cycle is the engine, then the five factors are the fuel.**

After discovering that only a tiny fraction of business leaders participate in peer advisory groups to raise their game, despite how unbelievably effective they are, I was inspired to describe what makes these groups tick. Doing so, I believed, would provide another option for CEOs to consider, along with reading books, hiring coaches, and attending executive development programs at major universities. The thought here was to shine a brighter light on this opportunity—not just to benefit Vistage but for a whole host of other organizations who lead such groups (YPO, EO, TAB, Renaissance, etc.). That's what triggered writing *The Power of Peers*.

During our research for the book, we identified two concepts that are central to this narrative:

1. The learning-achieving cycle, noted in the introduction, was a dynamic we found to be evident in high-performing groups and, as I learned later, in high-performing teams. This is the engine that drives high performance and continuous improvement.
2. If the learning-achieving cycle is the engine, then the five factors are the fuel. The cycle doesn't just happen by throwing a bunch of people in a room and hoping for the best. It requires the five factors, which were initially presented as five pillars and in later years as a reinforcing loop. It's presented here to appreciate all the relationships and interdependencies that were uncovered during four years of workshops.[14]

Figure 4. The Five Factors

The five factors that created the framework for this narrative start with (1) having the right people in the room who share a clarity of purpose. These people must also enjoy 2) psychological safety, (3) be committed to being highly productive, (4) have a sense of personal responsibility/accountability to the team members, and (5) be led by a servant leader who serves as the steward of the other four factors. This book will unpack these factors to demonstrate how peer advantage drives Peernovation.

This brings me to my time at Mullen (today MullenLowe), an advertising agency headquartered in Boston. I was there for less than a year, largely because I was a bit burned out and had simply accepted one agency gig too many. That said, I have enormous respect for what they do and how they do it. They employ gifted professionals who challenge one another every day in pursuit of creating the best advertising in the world. They confront complex challenges under difficult time constraints with the same level of urgency and commitment to excellence that the NASA team demonstrated during the flight of Apollo 13. These teams encapsulate what high-performing teams are capable of, which raises this question: Why wouldn't we all want to be part of the highest performing team possible?

We do. Of course we do. We just don't always know what such a team looks like or how we could be a positive contributor to it. Turns out, being a member of a high-performing group or team is not a spectator sport.

A high-performing *we* begins with *me*.

Systems Thinking and What Peernovation Looks Like

Systems are all around us. While we tend to think in siloes (because that's what we were taught), we actually live in systems. The human body is a complex system. In recent years, there's been a great deal of conversation about how our gut health impacts our brain health. This notion is not a particularly intuitive connection for most of us. For me, it prompts questions about what other connections we are not thinking about and how that information could help us understand our bodies even better.

The world is another complex system. We witnessed the impact of reintroducing wolves to Yellowstone National Park; this act triggered countless changes in the ecosystem and eventually altered the course of the area's rivers.[15] Shelter in place orders in response to the coronavirus, across the US and around the world, have had far-reaching economic, environmental, and human ripple effects that most people regard as having taken place rather quickly.

Your company is also a complex system. One policy change in a specific department could inadvertently cause long-term damage to other areas of the organization. Sometimes, the damage can be seen immediately, while at other times, the impact is delayed to such an extent that it becomes difficult to trace it back to the source. You have to be wired to look for it. The more people you have doing it together, the more likely you'll avoid damage to the whole. This is why teams that collaborate effectively to see the big picture and think in terms of systems are so important.

Albert Einstein once said, "We can't solve problems by using the same kind of thinking we used when we created them."[16] Systems thinking, a framework for studying interrelationships and patterns of change rather than objects or moments in time, was popularized by Peter Senge in his 1990 book, *The Fifth Discipline: The Art & Practice of the Learning Organization*. Systems thinking had been evolving rapidly since the end of World War II. Starting with hard systems thinking, as the existence of gaps between performance and goals for well-defined problems, it eventually evolved to soft systems thinking, where the world is viewed as inherently problematic and ambiguous, thus requiring a higher level of inquiry to understand a problem. From this evolution, a key idea emerged: that models developed as a result of past experiences could be created to address future situations.[17] The modeling of the 1970s set the stage for the development and utilization of systems archetypes in the 1980s and 1990s.[18] These archetypes identify common occurrences and circumstances that emerge, providing a framework that can be useful for both diagnosis and planning purposes.[19] If one considers the elements of systems thinking (reinforcing and balancing loops) as nouns and verbs, then systems archetypes (models) serve as the sentences and stories.[20]

There are roughly ten common systems archetypes that illustrate problems and frame opportunities inherent in both organizations and society. The systems archetypes covered here, for illustration purposes only, were applied to two scenarios at Vistage Worldwide during my time there. They are Limits to Growth and Tragedy of the Commons.

Limits to Growth

Limits to Growth was introduced in 1972 by Donella Meadows, Dennis Meadows, Jorgen Randers, and William Behrens.[21] This archetype illustrates the point that all reinforcing loops or activities will at some point confront a balancing loop, or force driven by a limiting factor. A popular product may sell so well that sales outpace production capacity, causing delays in replenishing inventories and thus slowing sales. A professional services firm in a small city that promises to hire only the best consultants may be able to find this talent locally at first, but if the firm continues to grow, the local talent pool will likely dry up, forcing either the recruitment of second-tier talent or looking outside the market.

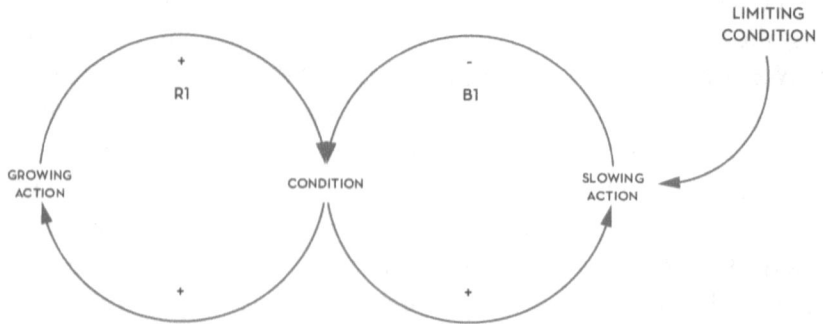

Figure 5. Limits to Growth (Braun 2002; Senge 2006)

The limiting condition (production capability or local talent pool) shown in figure 5 fuels the slowing action of the balancing loop (the pace of sales or the ability to hire locally) thus affecting the momentum of the reinforcing loop. To solve for this problem, Senge's 2006 book, *The Fifth Discipline,* recommends addressing the limiting condition rather than focusing on the reinforcing loop. While driving the reinforcing loop may yield short-term results, the limiting factor remains, revealing the truth of Senge's law number 4: "Behavior grows better before it grows worse."[22]

Tragedy of the Commons

In December 1968, ecologist Garrett Hardin introduced the Tragedy of the Commons archetype. Hardin described the tragedy as the abuse of finite resources available to the population as a whole, without regard for the whole population. Such abuses can result in weakening or even destroying common resources for survival, whether it's food, water, energy, or land.[23] Its application to organizations manifests when everyone uses a single, limited resource within that organization, yet individuals consider it their personal resource without regard for the demands being placed upon it by the entire organization. When this resource becomes overload, it can result in mistakes, delays, eroding trust, and loss of confidence.

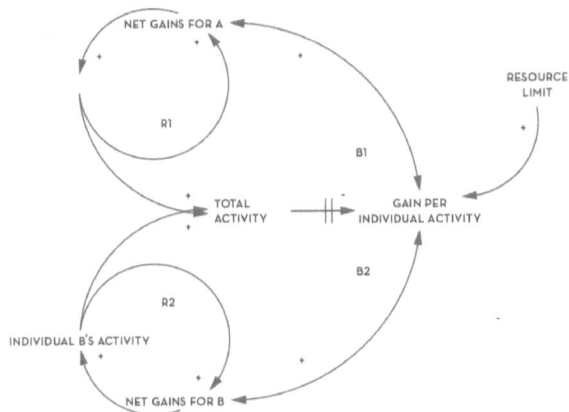

Figure 6. Tragedy of the Commons (Braun 2002; Senge 2006)

A common resource often has limitations, whether it's the number of people available or the amount of money budgeted to fund that resource. How many of you work in a company where you have a marketing or IT department that gets overwhelmed by service requests? Because marketing and IT prove so valuable to the individuals who access it, they are driven to use it more frequently, without regard for the larger picture (everyone else making service requests), causing a strain in the ability to keep pace with the demand. Solving for problems of the commons involves bringing everyone together, making them aware of the situation, and devising strategies and schedules that will ease the burden.[24]

Putting Systems Thinking to Work

During my time at Vistage Worldwide (2010–2016), we used systems thinking archetypes to identify strategies for accelerating revenue growth and for planning for the successful implementation of these strategies. The following examples offer a look at how the archetype Limits to Growth was used to diagnose a specific problem and identify a major strategy for unlocking the organization's true potential. Executing that strategy, however, would have major implications on the marketing department. Tragedy of the Commons provided early warning signs of what those pressures would look like and how best to address them.

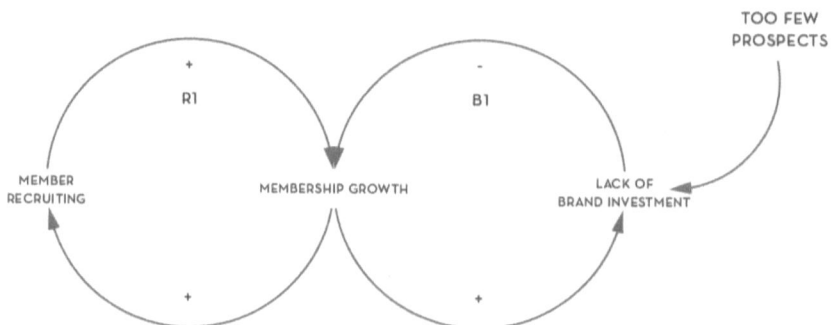

Figure 7. Limits to Growth (new members)

The Limits to Growth archetype provided a model that would drive a longer-term solution for achieving scalable, sustainable, and predictable growth. Rather than redouble its member recruiting efforts, the leadership addressed the limiting condition (lack of brand awareness/investment). This involved undertaking a rebranding initiative that created a stronger identity and better understanding of the value proposition among its target audiences, thus inspiring more CEOs and business leaders to join its groups in greater numbers.

Employing Tragedy of the Commons for Planning

Since there were roughly twenty internal clients at Vistage responsible for leading various initiatives within the business, each of these twenty clients would need to call upon marketing to rebrand all of its offline and online marketing materials. These clients each had bonus incentives tied to SMART goals (Specific, Measurable, Attainable, Results-Oriented, Time-bound). This resulted in a tendency to regard their projects as the most important projects to the company at any given time, with little consideration for other company needs. This common resource came under strain at least twice a year when several marketing campaigns from different departments converged at the same time. The Tragedy of the Commons archetype illustrates the problem.

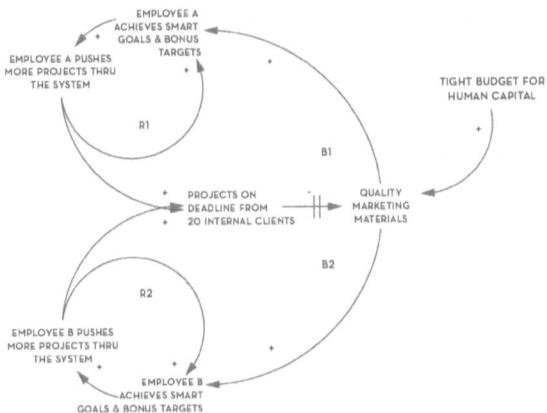

Figure 8. Tragedy of the Commons (marketing)

In figure 8, note that the resource limit isn't simply related to having enough people; it's also about budget. At the time, Vistage hired independent contractors to assist the marketing team during the busiest times of the year. Adding to staff or hiring more contractors to manage the volume of work required to deliver rebranded materials to every department in the company by year-end, however, was not an option. In the past, the team simply suffered the long hours and deadline pressures, accepting it as just part of the job, realizing that there would be an end in sight. It was one of the biggest reasons this tragedy had not been addressed in the past.

Addressing the Problem

After sharing the Tragedy of the Commons model with the marketing team, we conducted interviews with the director, creative manager, and project scheduler. In a group interview setting, each was asked a series of questions that explored what would happen if the team simply weathered the storm, as the department typically does, despite realizing that the incoming storm would be worse than anything they had ever experienced. The project scheduler was worried about missing deadlines and having to confront angry internal clients who may think her priorities were unfair to them. The creative manager was deeply concerned about the ability to deliver such a high volume of work and maintain quality, stating, "As we launch the new brand and introduce it to everyone, how can we possibly contemplate anything that would compromise the quality of that effort?" The director noted that if clients believed their projects could not be completed in a timely fashion, they would find their own resources to do the work, thus sacrificing quality control.

Now What? Where's the Leverage?

Managing this common resource would involve educating all the participants and employing peer-to-peer accountability and self-regulation, to be designed by the participants, as a means of managing the resource for everyone's individual and collective benefit.[25] Improving one's understanding of what their coworkers do is often an essential first step.[26] With that in mind, the team proposed the following solutions:

1. Create a win-win environment.
2. Ask the clients to be mindful that they are one of twenty, not one of one.
3. Explore ways to streamline marketing processes for the clients.
4. Create transparency through an online quarterly calendar that's accessible for all internal clients so they have a complete picture of what's ahead for the commons.
5. Establish a creative showcase, both online and in the office, where the creative pieces developed in collaboration with each of the clients are showcased to inspire everyone's commitment to producing excellent work under the new brand banner.
6. Schedule monthly meetings to review all projects in the pipeline and for the ninety-day period following the meeting so that expectations for requests and deadlines are clear and to give the clients a voice.
7. Set up a kick-off meeting that includes all the clients to frame the challenge, present some initial ideas for solutions, obtain feedback and ideas, and develop a plan together, one that meets both individual needs and organizational brand imperatives.
8. To keep the meeting positive and upbeat, the team has named this project "The Success of the Commons," with the tagline: "Strategy to avoid the tragedy." The hope was to inspire everyone's commitment to a positive result for all.

Coincidentally, a revised bonus structure that was instituted by the new CEO was based more on organizational performance than the achievement of individual SMART goals, setting the stage for a more collaborative environment. Now, everyone's success mattered to each individual employee that much more.

This is an illustration of Peernovation at its finest. Not surprisingly, Peernovation is not a linear idea; it's a system unto itself. It works when people are committed to collaborating and cooperating, recognizing that they need each other to be successful. When these people broaden their view, understand the whole, and express ideas that result in a better way of working, those ideas tend to be sustainable.

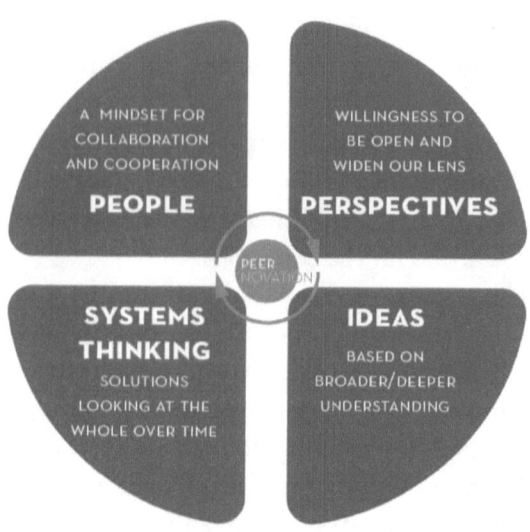

Figure 9. Peernovation in action

Systems archetypes not only help diagnose problems and uncover underlying issues; they also offer a framework for anticipating impending situations and exploring how to exercise leverage in time for effective implementation.

Peernovation as an Iterative Process

One might consider a team of CEOs to be a formidable adversary against a team of directors or managers. Formidable, sure. Unbeatable, not at all. Are you familiar with the Marshmallow Challenge?[27] It's been around for a while as a popular team-building exercise to see which team of four can build the tallest structure in eighteen minutes, using twenty sticks of spaghetti, a yard of string, a yard of tape, a measuring tape, and a marshmallow. The catch is that the marshmallow must sit at the top of the structure. It's not unlike what the NASA team was challenged to do, at least from the perspective that time was of the essence, and they had limited materials available to them to achieve the goal.

You may be surprised to learn which types of teams typically outperform the others in the Marshmallow Challenge. CEOs outperform recent business school graduates, but kindergartners outperform them both. CEOs and business school students tend to place a great deal of emphasis on planning, only to run tight on time when it comes to building the actual structure. By the time they put the marshmallow on top, if the tower topples over, they have little chance to recover. Kindergartners don't approach the task with any preconceived ideas that can take them down the wrong path. They don't concern themselves with planning or fighting over who's in charge, so they take a more iterative, trial-and-error approach. On average, they are outperformed only by teams of architects and engineers. (Given that the challenge speaks to a basic understanding of structure, feel free to breathe a sigh of relief.)

> **CEOs outperform recent business school graduates, but kindergartners outperform them both.**

Who is on the team matters, but not for the attributes you might consider most important. It's not about intellect or individual talent; it's about how the team members are wired to work together. People who are willing to collaborate, who learn from their colleagues, who share ideas based on what they've learned, and who are committed to genuinely meeting a challenge together are by far the best teams.

WHERE PEERNOVATION CAME FROM

In August 2012, I wrote a piece titled "Peernovation" that recalled a definition I had once read for innovation as "creativity realized."[28] I thought it squared nicely with some comments Simon Sinek had raised during one of his webinars, including some observations that speak to why peer advisory groups and teams have a unique capacity for inspiring innovation.

First, new ideas are more likely to come from outside your industry than inside it. Throw away your industry trade pubs, where everyone is saying the same thing, and look at what's happening elsewhere to see what you can apply to your own work. Industry-diverse groups and teams are hardwired for apprehending information and insights from other sectors.

Second, innovation is best discovered in groups of three. If you see the typical peer advisory group or team as a triad, as I do, it involves 1) the leader/facilitator; 2) the group; and 3) the individual member. Together, they create the magic.

Assemble the right collection of people who are clear about what they want to accomplish, will leverage the law of three, and fearlessly create and implement their own solutions, and you've got Peernovation.

Chapter Summary

The Apollo 13 story lets us imagine the life-or-death stakes, the time pressure, the limited materials, and the challenge of communicating a solution with no visuals that could be executed by crew members more than two hundred thousand miles away. How would your team fare under those circumstances? If they took the Marshmallow Challenge, would they perform more like the kindergartners or the business school students?

The learning-achieving cycle that drives most high-performing groups and teams doesn't happen by accident. It requires 1) having the right people committed to a common purpose; 2) a culture of psychological safety that celebrates transparency, asking good questions, and taking risks; 3) systems and processes that drive productivity; 4) people who believe their currency rests largely with their fellow team members; and 5) leaders who are there to support the success of the team and who keep a watchful eye on the status of the other four factors.

Reacquainting ourselves with systems thinking (and how archetypes can help us solve problems) when you have dedicated people, willing to do everything it takes to address challenges and opportunities at their root causes, is a worthwhile pursuit.

Consider starting an efficient and scalable business that might have helped the Lovells with their after-party cleanup. It would undoubtedly be appreciated by an incalculable number of people you could save from having to sell their homes.

What's Next?

Start by thinking about connecting the dots in your life that give you special insights into the way you think about teams and how you can be a better team leader/member. If a better we begins with a better you, then what will you do? Chapter 2 will examine what having the right people on the team means and provide additional details that may help you answer that very question.

CHAPTER 2
The Right People

> The strength of the team is each individual member.
> The strength of each member is the team.[29]
> —Phil Jackson

IN THE INTRODUCTION, I ASKED YOU THE SAME QUESTION I ASK CEOs and key executives during my workshop: "What's the best team you've ever been part of and why?" I shared some of the responses I typically receive and suggested you give some thought to how you might answer. If I had to reply to that question, I wouldn't have to go back to Little League baseball. I've had the good fortune to be part of many amazing teams during my career. I will, however, go back thirty years to a team that is special to me because of the individuals involved, the approach we chose, the unlikelihood of success, and the result we achieved. It was the GTECH pitch team during my time at Wooding & Housley, a Providence-based advertising agency.

As the story goes, GTECH (now IGT, the dominant player in the lottery business) was putting its advertising account up for review. It was based in Rhode Island and planned to conduct get-acquainted meetings with six local agencies. A few of us approached our agency principals to suggest we put our hat in the ring and participate in the review. We received a firm no, stating that we didn't know anyone at GTECH, knew nothing about its business, and shouldn't engage in an expensive agency review we had little chance of winning. Not to mention, our client roster consisted mainly of industrial companies.

Hard to argue with that rationale, so we took our disappointment to a local pub. The "we" I'm talking about included Jim McGinn, account supervisor; Brian Murphy, art director; Todd Diamond, copywriter, and me, the PR guy. About three beers in and still unable to let go of our desire to pitch the GTECH business, we committed to approaching the principals on the following morning.

As a united front, we asked, "If we could squeeze our way into the review, could we pitch the business for the agency on our own time?"

They responded with a smirk but said, "Sure, knock yourselves out."

I don't recall which one of us secured our spot to participate in the review, but once we were in, we were committed to win. While we really wanted to capture the business, we were especially driven to doing everything possible to avoid the inevitable "I told you so" if we didn't prevail. The thing is, the agency principals were right. We were a huge underdog here, for the reasons they mentioned and many more. With that in mind, we got to work.

First, we agreed that we needed to do more in our meeting than just get acquainted. Second, we didn't know anyone at the company, so we knew our first impression was crucial. Third, realizing we knew nothing about their business, all four members of our ad hoc pitch team committed to digging up anything we could find about the company, and we had less than two weeks to do it.

This is where the timing of this story becomes even more relevant. It's not like we could go online and uncover a mountain of company, competitor, and industry data in a matter of hours. We had to identify relevant associations, obtain industry trade pubs, and find media clips, all of which had to be mailed to us. As I remember it, at the end of the week, we had this pile of info spread out on a conference room table – roughly 500 pages. Each of us committed to reading every word of it by Monday morning. Our meeting with the GTECH team was scheduled for just three days later.

By Monday morning, everyone had done their homework, as promised. We believed that having one person take the lead wouldn't cut it. Everyone on the team had to demonstrate their understanding of the landscape. But how? At first, we planned to show the client everything we read in preparation for our meeting. We thought that if they could see how much work we did, it would separate us from the rest. Eventually, we agreed that it was more important to show them what we didn't know than what we did. Counterintuitive, perhaps, but here's how we decided to approach the meeting.

> **Everyone on the team had to demonstrate their understanding of the landscape.**

We hosted the ninety-minute meeting (the last of the get-acquainted meetings) on a Thursday morning. After a brief agency tour, the four of us gathered the GTECH team in our conference room. The walls were lined with our creative work, the outside tables were topped with awards, and the conference table had a large pitcher of water, water glasses, coasters, yellow pads, and pencils at every chair. That's it. We stuffed all of the research materials we had amassed into desk drawers in an adjacent office and didn't refer to a single note during the meeting.

After everyone introduced themselves and the prospect shared what he believed to be the company's biggest challenge going forward, we started to ask questions. Not the kinds of questions one could find in the research material, but an entirely different level of questions, well-informed questions. While they were questions in search of answers, they were designed to demonstrate a high level of understanding of GTECH's business, competitors, new products, and so on. An hour later, with every member of our team engaged in this exchange, the marketing director slammed his pencil on the conference room table and shouted, "How in the world do you know so much about our business?"

If you're familiar with the term hanging curveball, the head of marketing just threw us one. While I don't remember which member of our team proceeded to hit that pitch out of the stadium, it was quite the moment. For me, it ranks right up there with the scene from *A Few Good Men* when Colonel Jessup (Jack Nicholson) responded to Lieutenant Caffey's (Tom Cruise) question about whether he ordered the code red by blurting out, "You're God damn right I did!"[30] We led the prospect right where we wanted him to go.

Shortly after the meeting concluded, they asked if we could continue our conversation over lunch. We took them to Capriccio, a northern Italian restaurant just a short walk away - a setting that's as good as it gets if you want to close a deal. Shortly after lunch, we received a call. We were hoping to hear that we advanced to the next round of the review. Instead, they told us that their search was over. We won the GTECH business.

THE TEAM

Now that you've read the story, what does it tell you about the people who made that client pitch? Could any four people have achieved the same result? Let's look at some of the common attributes of the team and its members:

1. **We enjoyed being together.** Our personal camaraderie and mutual respect for one another mattered a great deal. It was the foundation of our psychological safety and our ability to be straight with one another at all times. We enjoyed each other's company, which is why instead of going home after the agency principals told us no about pitching the GTECH business, we took the time to process that refusal together, over a beer. No trip to the pub, no pitch.

    > *Could any four people have achieved the same result?*

2. **We didn't know any better.** Or we had healthy egos, believing that if we set our minds to it, we'd perform like water; we would find a way. I'm pretty sure our resolve was fueled by a healthy combination of both. In the face of a perfectly logical argument to forget about going after the GTECH business, we pressed the matter and pursued the account with reckless abandon.
3. **We shared leadership.** It wasn't that there was no leader as much as we trusted each other's specific competencies so much that it was pretty clear who should take the lead at any given juncture. We all stepped up when it made sense, a little bit like kindergartners.
4. **We realized our currency rested with how we showed up for each other.** Pursuing our shared goal, which we refused to be

denied, would require each of us to bring our A games to every aspect of the challenge. For example, it never occurred to any one of us not to complete the five hundred pages of reading we promised to each other to do. We were all in.

5. **We learned better together.** The magic happened when we shared what we learned with one another, after our massive reading assignment. Since each of us was seeing the content through our respective mental models, the more we talked, the more we discovered knowledge from facts and uncovered ideas from data.

6. **We were committed to taking a risk.** Now that you know how the story ends, it may not sound that risky to host a client meeting with no formal presentation and blank yellow pads. However, based on the fact that the other agencies had already shaped the prospect's expectations for our meeting, it wasn't so clear to us. That said, suffice it to say we learned a great deal about the value of asking the right questions.

7. **We were lucky.** We could have just as easily blown it. Still, if you define luck as the confluence of opportunity and preparation, we created the opportunity and took nothing for granted in our preparation. In our minds, even if we were not selected, we took our best shot and would have been perfectly happy to live with that, the result notwithstanding.

> *As a team, though, we believed we could do anything.*

8. **We had talented individuals committed to being good teammates.** This may be the most essential attribute of all. If you look at the individuals involved compared to the people and resources invested by the other agencies, you would know that a betting person would never have squandered perfectly good money on us. As a team, though, we believed we could do anything.

As for talent, we were all at the dawn of our careers, so in the scheme of things, we didn't know if we were talented or not. Jim McGinn was a master at analytics and delivering exceptional client service. Jim would go on to enjoy an incredible career at some of the world's most notable ad shops. Brian Murphy would eventually leave Wooding & Housley to lead Hill Holiday Design, where he created logos and built brand platforms for some of the world's largest organizations and educational institutions. Copywriter Todd Diamond, who once asked Linda Blair to autograph her publicity photo for him with the line, "Todd, you make my head spin," is a gifted writer, who today owns his own firm. The PR business was good to me as well, as I ran the gamut from running my own shop to working for one of the world's largest multinational agencies.

Teams are like snowflakes: No two are the same, so having the right people on the team who will get the job done matters. While you need people with the right skills and work ethic, they also have to be the kind of people who understand that the team is bigger and more capable than any individual. In a nutshell, based on my research with groups and teams, here are the three categories for what having the right people looks like:

Common Purpose

All group and team members should be aligned and deeply committed to why they are there and what they expect to achieve for themselves and their teammates. For a CEO peer group, it may translate into CEOs who want to engage other CEOs (people who share their unique position of responsibility) in a manner that will help them make better decisions, grow as leaders, and maximize the performance of their organizations. For a sports team, it may mean doing what it takes to win a national championship; for a business, it may be creating the best advertising in the world.

Shared Values and Behaviors

While common purpose is a critical guidepost, not everyone shares the same sensibilities about what it takes to be a great teammate or exhibits behaviors congruent with their espoused values. This speaks to culture.

The more we dive into Peernovation, the more you'll discover why it has been developed as a framework and not a prescription for high-performing groups and teams. Who am I to tell you what your ideal group or team should look like? If you've ever wondered how some people can be really successful on a team in one work environment and why that same person can be so unsuccessful somewhere else, this is why.

Diversity and Inclusion

The first two components speak to similarities we should share, while diversity and inclusion refer to the importance of differences and why they matter so much. Diversity and inclusion are where we broaden our perspective. Think of diversity in every possible way: race, gender, religious beliefs, gender identification, age, work history, education, hometown, and so on. If we select age for a moment, consider that we're at the start of having five different generations in today's workforce fueled by the emergence of Generation Z and people forgoing traditional retirement by working into their seventies (and eighties). While each generation shares a common humanity, the way they see the world has been shaped by entirely different events and experiences. The more we are willing to learn rather than judge, the more perspectives we can reveal. The more inclusive and respectful we are, the more effective our teams will become.

Linking These Ideas to My Peernovation Workshop

When you consider the money and time business leaders invest in their peer groups, it's imperative for me to help them squeeze every ounce of value possible from each meeting (as well as during the weeks in between). The more work I did with groups, the more I saw the relevance of this exercise for cross-functional work teams (and any team, for that matter).

The half-day workshop for teams involves a brief presentation on how peer influence in our personal lives and in the workplace can help us rethink the way we communicate in our organizations. I talk about peer advantage, the learning-achieving cycle, Peernovation, and the five factors that make it all possible.

For a peer group, the members will define and shape how the other four factors (psychological safety, productivity, accountability, and leadership) are exhibited. If a group has a good handle on what these four factors should look like and how they can drive success, they can be more specific when it comes to developing the criteria used to screen new members. As part of the workshop, we ask the members if we have all the right people in the room based on the attributes outlined previously: common purpose, shared values and behaviors, and diversity.

For teams, this framework allows for a great deal of flexibility for determining the right people for the team and the values and behaviors they should exhibit. In doing so, it shines a bright light on team priorities. Well-defined priorities help leaders determine who to add to the team someday, while guiding current team members to identify the expectations they have of themselves and others today and in the future.

During this segment, it can be particularly helpful to ask the question, What's the difference between the people who succeed in our organization (or on this team) and those who do not? To add some context here, because I've hired many people in my career, let's see if you can relate to this experience.

I would review an incredible resume and then invite the candidate for an interview with me and several team members. The conversations would go beautifully, and we would hire the candidate to join the team, only to discover three months down the road that we made a big mistake. When I share this scenario with CEOs in their peer group meetings, they all nod in agreement when it comes to having had that experience. As we know, it doesn't necessarily mean that the people we hired were terrible, they were just a bad fit for us.

So asking your team members what they believe it takes to make it on *this* team can be very enlightening. Since getting this task right can mean the difference between incremental growth and exponential growth (or even success and failure), the mantra of hiring slowly and firing quickly reveals a certain wisdom. In chapter 7, I'll cover common challenges and provide some tools to address them when it comes to what having the right people looks like for you.

UNDERSTANDING PEER INFLUENCE IS CRITICAL

The pervasive nature of peer influence is undeniable. There are countless studies on the subject, but you don't need a pile of reports to tell you what your life has shown you time and time again. The people around you have influenced you for as long as you can remember. Your parents likely cared about who you selected as friends when you were growing up, and for a good reason. They understood all too well how the people who surround us can drag us down, hold us at bay, and lift us up. They realized that quotes such as: "We're all in the same boat," "Great minds think alike," and "Bird of feather flock together" are more than just common expressions.

We influence one another as adults as well. We rely on our peers, coworkers, and family members to help us discover meaning in whatever situation we may find ourselves. Whether we want to buy a book or a car, we look beyond what the manufacturer and professional reviewers have to say. We seek out our peers to learn about their experiences and findings. Interestingly enough, when we do so online, we accept the prevailing sentiment of the crowd as a powerful data point in our decision-making process, even though we may not know any of the individuals offering their opinions. We also look to our peers at work. According to the 2019 Edelman Trust Barometer,[31] we trust our coworkers more than the CEO, senior leadership team, or the board of directors when it comes to making sense of what's happening at the company and determining what it means for the employees. Our peers matter, and they matter huge.

> **Peer•no•va•tion**
> **(pir-nə-'vā-shən)**
> **combines the words peer (people like me) and innovation (creativity realized).**

Since peer influence is such a powerful and pervasive force, it stands to reason that we should learn to maximize it. The road from peer influence to peer advantage is simple but not easy. It's simple because it's all about being intentional. If you can be more selective, strategic, and structured about the people you surround yourself with, you'll begin to experience the benefits of peer advantage.

Peer•no•va•tion (pir-nə-'vā-shən) combines the words *peer* (people like me) and *innovation* (creativity realized). As stated previously, Peernovation is what happens when a group of people who share common values, yet offer different perspectives and skills, bring ideas to life. Here is where peer advantage bears fruit.

As Ken Blanchard said, "None of us is as smart as all of us," and none of us is as creative as all of us, either.[32] I've been fortunate on countless occasions to have led and been a member of teams who produced outstanding work for our clients. Any member of any of these teams (me included, of course) would readily admit that no individual could have ever come up with the same high level of work if left to their own devices. Put a group of talented people with different skills sets and experiences in a room, and if they are relentless about achieving a quality outcome, watch out. Teams like these are what separate great companies from good ones.

> **It's what runs horizontally that gives strength and stability to what's vertical**

Achieving Peernovation based solely on the intention of leveraging peer influence through peer advantage doesn't happen by accident. It requires all of us to recognize that an organization's potential doesn't lie in its top-down organizational structure. It's what runs horizontally that gives strength and stability to what's vertical, a force of nature that challenges us to set a higher standard of excellence for us all.

Chapter Summary

It all starts with having the right people who have clear expectations of their roles and how they can add value. Our team that pitched the GTECH business offers a simple illustration of what's possible. When team members embrace a common purpose, enjoy shared values and behaviors, and offer a diversity of skills and perspective with a view of the broader landscape, they are tough to beat.

Consider how the right people are at the core when it comes to your level of performance for the other four factors. Understanding how you want to perform in each of these areas will not only help you find who the right people are, but over time, it will drive your psychological safety, productivity, accountability, and leadership levels to new heights.

What's Next?

The Marshmallow Challenge offered us a glimpse into just one of the benefits of psychological safety. Kids outperform adults in this exercise because they'll try anything and are fearless when it comes to making mistakes. This iterative approach and the environment that encourages it is something that deserves our attention. There are other benefits to creating psychological safety as well. Chapter 3 will explore those benefits and discuss how to achieve them.

CHAPTER 3
Psychological Safety

> Teamwork begins by building trust. And the only way to
> do that is to overcome our need for invulnerability.[33]
> —Patrick Lencioni

WHEN I CONDUCTED MY FIRST HALF-DOZEN WORKSHOPS starting about four years ago, I asked CEO Peer Groups how they would rank their safe and confidential environment on a scale of 1–10. This was how I framed the psychological safety question for mastermind groups back then. I wanted them to think of it in terms of how willing they are to be transparent and how much they trust the confidentiality of the environment. Their belief that what happens in the room stays in the room is among the conditions that make members feel more comfortable to share.

The initial response I received to this question in the early days was typically 9.5 to 10. The members expressed an incredibly high degree of confidence in the safety of the environment. That said, as the workshop proceeded and the dialogue continued, I wasn't necessarily feeling that the candor of the conversation matched the high rankings members were ascribing to themselves. It finally dawned on me that I was asking the wrong question, or at least I needed to ask an additional one.

Today, I ask two questions: How would you rank your safe and confidential environment on a scale of 1–10? And how would you rate your ability to leverage that environment on a scale of 1–10? The answer to the first question remains in the 9–10 range; the answer to the second question dips to an average of 6.5. In asking the second question, I paint a picture for them. I ask them to imagine they are at a beautiful spa, looking at a gorgeous pool of water, with steam gently rising off the surface. They know if they immerse themselves in the pool, it will be among the most relaxing, restorative experiences they've ever had. Yet some of them, rather than immerse themselves in the pool, will be content to sit in a nearby lounge chair, reading a magazine or merely dangling their feet in the water. Knowing the group environment is safe or that the pool will be amazing is one thing; being willing to reap its full benefits is quite another.

For CEO peer groups, consider the fact that in large part, having a safe place to confer with fellow CEOs is one of the most important reasons they join a group. For most of them, it's the only place they can go where they don't have to put their best face forward, where they can express their uncertainty and fears in an environment among peers willing to do the same. It's how they help each other grow.

Having the right people is essential, and their proficiency in creating and leveraging a safe environment is what unlocks their ability to perform at a high level. It doesn't mean they have to be perfect at it, as long as they are willing to improve on their ability to access whatever is inside them to leverage the safe environment more effectively. And because we as peers tend to influence one another's behavior, the more each individual improves, the more likely each person gets better at it to everyone's benefit.

> **Teams work together to achieve a collective goal or create a shared work product.**

The Difference between Groups and Teams

As stated in the introduction, groups convene to help their members achieve their goals. Teams work together to achieve a collective goal or create a shared work product. As a result, psychological safety in groups and organizations tends to play out a bit differently.

In a group, for example, safety covers three areas: 1) a member's willingness to be open with the group about what's happening in their business and their life that could impact their ability to achieve the goals they have stated for themselves; 2) a trust that confidentiality is sacrosanct, along with the tacit agreement that nothing discussed during the meeting ever gets talked about outside the meeting, unless the members agree that it is permissible to do so; and 3) an environment that allows for members to support and respectfully challenge one another, recognizing that such a challenge is delivered with positive intent in the sole interest of the member who is being challenged.

In an organizational team situation, it tends to focus on whether the culture invites people to ask questions, express ideas, or take risks free of embarrassment or even punishment by leaders and other team members. Do they speak up or stay silent? Do they play to win or just to keep from losing?

Group Story

In early 2017, I led a workshop for a group of CEOs in the Midwest; this group had been in existence for nearly twenty years. You can imagine my trepidation about delivering my workshop to people who had so much experience working together. They had helped each other thrive during the good times and survive the challenging ones. They knew each other incredibly well and believed they had a pretty good handle on what a capable group should look like. What could they get out of my workshop that they had not already addressed?

Keep in mind that the added value to the group workshop is that I also provide members with all the material necessary to lead a similar exercise with teams back at their organizations. To them, I positioned it much more in terms of participating as a group as a way to stick their hands in the clay, so they could better empathize with what the exercise might feel like for their people. I also made the point that this is a self-assessment. I wasn't there to tell them what their group norms should be. I'm just sharing a framework to guide them with fine-tuning what they want for themselves. The good news is (and I've found this consistently over the past four years), the stronger the group, the higher their expectations of one another and the value they wish to receive. They tend to set their own standard of excellence; it's quite impressive to watch.

To that end, something happened during the meeting I did not expect. This group was among those that prompted me, later on, to ask groups not just whether their environment was safe, but how capable the individuals in the group were at leveraging it. After the initial presentation and an in-depth conversation about what having the right people looks like, we moved on to a safe and confidential environment. Their response to the question about whether they enjoyed an open environment where confidentiality was sacrosanct and to rank it on a scale of 1–10 was a resounding 10. Rather than let that go, we talked about it for a while because I was interested in learning how they achieved it and what specifically made them feel that way.

During this conversation, one member said, "You know, I would agree with everyone for the most part, but let's face it, there's the elephant in the room. Or to be more accurate, the elephant not in the room."

It so happened that about six months earlier, one of the group's longtime, respected members (I'll call him John) made a unilateral decision to skip the morning portion of the group meeting, which almost always included a featured speaker. After more than a decade with the group, John felt like he had heard it all. While he still gained tremendous value from the deep conversations among members that would take place in the afternoon executive session, he opted to skip the morning and only be an afternoon participant. Because John was quite influential, other members began to follow suit, which explains why there were only nine members at my workshop instead of the full sixteen.

As you might imagine, this fact began to surface during our initial conversation about having all the right people in the room. This sparked a more in-depth conversation because members who continued to come to the morning speaker session were starting to resent those who did not. No one liked it, but they didn't know what to do about it. John was such a valuable afternoon contributor that there was some hesitancy in raising the issue with him directly. The argument from some was, we'd rather have him here half the time than not at all. Concerned that he might leave the group if they confronted him, they tabled the conversation, at least for the moment. As the workshop entered its phases of productivity, accountability, and leadership, it became clear that the group (or at least a few of its representatives) resolved to address their concerns with John directly.

About a week later, a few of the members approached John with their concern. Turns out John felt terrible that he had set an example to others that the morning portion of the meeting was optional. John not only happily reengaged full-time but also encouraged the members who had previously followed his lead to do so as well.

This was a positive outcome of a situation that may have eventually reached a boiling point, possibly fracturing the group and compromising its long-term viability. The values of the members prevailed and provided them the courage to address the matter directly. They cast aside their assumptions about what might go wrong and chose to trust that everyone would eventually act in a manner that served the whole, not any individual member. It was in this spirit that John was approached and also how he responded. Honest conversation among people of shared values won the day, as it usually does.

> **Honest conversation among people of shared values won the day, as it usually does.**

The Value of Honest Conversation

Healthy, deep conversations not only inspire psychological safety and trust, but they also create a context for better decision-making. Conversely, if the environment is not psychologically safe, then it makes having such conversations nearly impossible. A great example of why conversations matter is evident in academic research that parses the difference between indifference and ambivalence.[34] At first blush, we might consider this as an argument of semantics versus substance, a distinction without a difference, if you will. Yet there's a big difference. A neutral response to an employee survey question, for example, could either indicate indifference or ambivalence. Without the ability to discern between the two, the researcher wonders whether employees simply don't care (indifference) or care a great deal but struggle with conflicting emotions (ambivalence).

To illustrate this point, let's say a company plans to move its offices thirty miles away. The employees may be thrilled about the prospect of moving into new office space but dread the idea of a longer commute. If a company announces a layoff, the employees who keep their jobs may be grateful. Yet they may also be upset by losing some coworkers and possibly angry at the company's leadership team, particularly if no one on that team lost their job or took a pay cut. When silence is assumed to be indifference, we can't find out what's going on unless we suspend our assumptions, create an environment where it's safe for employees to voice their opinions, and care enough to ask (repeatedly).

I became fascinated with this entire indifference/ambivalence topic because of the range of implications and its particular relevance to psychological safety and decision-making in groups and teams. One of the significant advantages of advancing the study of ambivalence is that it's relevant to all human relationships, in every environment. It allows for experiencing the type of collateral learning that results when multiple disciplines contribute to a broader understanding of a subject.[35] Ambivalence can actually foster better personal decision-making because competing points of view are recognized and more readily accessible.[36]

Here are some questions for groups, teams, and their leaders: How can you have honest conversations at every level in the workplace? What would that involve? Here is where Craig Weber's work on conversational capacity can provide us additional guidance. According to Weber, it's about having the willingness and the ability to engage in conversations that involve a balance between candor and curiosity, something he calls the sweet spot.[37]

If people are afraid to speak their minds, it can result in low candor, where the conversation becomes overly guarded and cautious, if it happens at all. When there is low curiosity (because only their view matters), people tend to speak their minds at the expense of listening to others or trying to understand a situation beyond their own ladder of inference. In this case, conversations grow more arrogant and argumentative. When candor and

> **Building individual and team conversational capacity and creating psychological safety are interdependent if not synonymous.**

curiosity are both low, it's usually a product of indifference. The bottom line, however, is that you'll never know whether a person is indifferent or simply afraid to speak up about conflicting emotions or thoughts because of low candor. Building individual and team conversational capacity and creating psychological safety are interdependent if not synonymous.

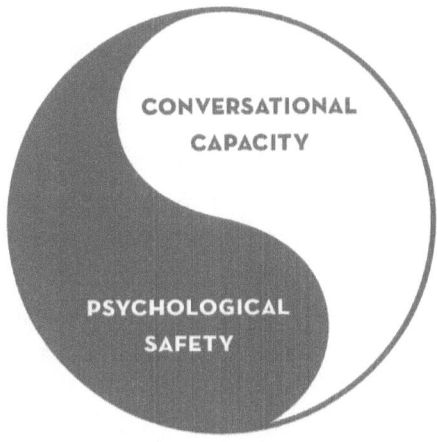

Figure 10. One inspires the other.

The following text offers some parameters for building the kind of trust and psychological safety that can make high levels of conversational capacity possible.

A Few Words about Trust

At the core of psychological safety is trust, which "involves the juxtaposition of people's loftiest hopes and aspirations with their deepest worries and fears."[38] On the one hand, we trust pilots to keep us safe, physicians to make us well, and other drivers to follow the rules of the road: people we don't know and would have relatively little understanding of their competence even if we did. We read reviews on Yelp, Amazon, and Consumer Reports from people who share a common interest in trendy restaurants, historical fiction, or luxury automobiles. We don't know these people from Adam, but we will accept their findings as essential data points when it comes to making our purchasing decisions. As the Edelman Trust Barometer has shown us over the years, the less we trust institutions, the more we look to one another. The less we believe in the reliability of social media, the more we look to those closest to us: our family, friends, and coworkers.

Yet trust as a member of a small group or team is often guided by the same mental models and assumptions described in the ladder of inference outlined in the introduction. They can run deep and are often difficult to identify and articulate, but suffice it to say that as a result, some people are naturally more comfortable being open. In contrast, others hold their ideas and feelings closer to the vest. Because of this dynamic, the definition of what it means to be open for one person can be entirely different from what it means to someone else. So if there's no universal standard for what being open and trusting looks like, then how do you know when you've achieved it? What does a 10 look like? Let's dig a little deeper.

Realizing Psychological Safety

Grasping an intellectual appreciation for the value of psychological safety in a group or team is one thing. Recognizing it and understanding what it takes to keep it is more challenging. It's especially true because everyone's definition, capacity, and natural inclination for trusting others and being truly open can be quite different. That's why keeping it at the forefront as something to be advanced and nurtured versus a fixed goal to be achieved is the first step.

The conditions and behaviors that members of groups and teams bring up most often regarding what it takes to experience psychological safety are as follows:

Mutual respect. Respecting one another as professionals and people who share common challenges and aspirations inside and outside the workplace is at the core. If there's no respect, there will be no trust.

Familiarity. Sounds obvious, but the better the team members know one another, the more comfortable they are with sharing and asking questions. Achieving the level of familiarity they are seeking rarely takes place at a monthly meeting or in the context of a typical workday. It requires getting to know one another over coffee, drinks, bowling, miniature golf, or at a retreat setting, where deeper, more personal conversations in smaller groups tend to take place. These shared experiences build trust and create stronger bonds.

Learn, not judge. When people are inclined to ask good questions and listen for understanding, as opposed to making assumptions and jumping to conclusions based on their hardwired mental models, it's a recipe for a safe environment. Asking questions with the intent to increase understanding inspires psychological safety. It doesn't mean you have to agree with one another; just be open to learning a different point of view from your own.

Model sharing behaviors. When members choose to be vulnerable and ask a question no one wants to ask, or when members share a personal feeling most people would keep to themselves, it provides a strong example for the others. It offers reassurance that if they were to share, there's not only no penalty for this action, but also a benefit to the entire group. Sharing ideas and asking uncomfortable questions are acts of courage and generosity. Courage because members put themselves out there, and generosity because of the benefit it provides everyone. Think about the example of the member who dared to point out "the elephant not in the room" and how much the group benefited from what eventually transpired.

> **Sharing ideas and asking uncomfortable questions are acts of courage and generosity.**

Model listening behaviors. Think of the illustration of the pool at the spa. The person getting into the pool is the one sharing; the pool itself represents the people who are listening. The more attentive and engaged they are, the more inviting the environment. It's the listeners who provide the safety. When it comes to safety, the difference between an audience who is locked in versus checking their cell phones or staring out a window is night and day.

Share experiences rather than advice. Unless specifically requested by a member, resist the temptation to tell people what they should or should not do. Instead, share experiences designed to help them reach their own conclusions. It makes the environment safer for sharing and allows for a member to own their action items, and when they do, they are more likely to act on them and follow through.

Be respectful and trust intent. Helping someone can often require tough love; challenging someone in an open meeting can be tricky. To do so, the group or team has to adopt this practice as an acceptable norm, one that is never aimed to call someone out at their expense, but only to serve as a means for helping the individual or the collective. For the person who believes the challenge is necessary, do so in a manner that's direct and respectful. For the member being challenged, despite how the challenge may come across in the moment, take a breath and remind yourself to trust the intent.

Maintaining Psychological Safety

Let's assume you lead a group or team that enjoys the benefit of a safe environment, one that encompasses all the conditions and behaviors that have been described. Maintaining it involves being attentive to it. As the leader (or any member, for that matter), the day you say, "We got this," and move on will be the day that safety is reduced. If you don't water a plant on a regular basis, it will die. Safe environments that are not constantly nurtured will do the same. Circumstances change. People change. As some people leave the group, new people join. Every time there's a change, the safety of the environment takes a hit. How do I know? If you ask the members, that's what they will tell you.

Chapter Summary

The question isn't just about whether the environment is safe; the question is also whether people are taking full advantage of the safe environment they have. Safety for groups and teams manifests a bit differently, yet they are both critically important. In a group, it's about the willingness of members to be open about what's happening in their business and their life that could impact their ability to achieve the goals they have stated for themselves. It involves a trust that confidentiality is sacrosanct and the tacit agreement that nothing discussed during the meeting ever gets talked about outside the meeting, unless the members agree that it is permissible to do so. It's also an environment that allows for members to support and respectfully challenge one another, recognizing that such a challenge is to be delivered with positive intent in the sole interest of the member being challenged.

In a team situation, it's about whether the context within which a team operates invites people to ask questions, express ideas, or take risks free of embarrassment or even punishment by leaders and other team members. Consider how difficult it can be to have honest conversations in the workplace and imagine the value of understanding the relationship between conversational capacity and psychological safety.

The conditions and behaviors necessary for psychological safety include mutual respect, familiarity, learning not judging, modeling sharing behaviors, modeling listening behaviors, sharing experiences rather than advice, being respectful, and trusting intent. The key to keeping psychological safety at a high level is to be relentlessly attentive to it.

What's Next?

Now that you have great people who trust each other and enjoy an environment of psychological safety, how do you maximize productivity? What does that look like for groups, and what does it mean for our teams? On to chapter 4.

CHAPTER 4
Productivity

> Great things in business are never done by one person; they're done by a team of people.[39]
> —Steve Jobs

PRODUCTIVITY IS AS MUCH ABOUT WHAT YOU ACCOMPLISH, AS IT is how you go about doing so. Take a look at most companies today. They set big goals and establish clear outcome metrics, but too often, they fail to carefully measure the outputs responsible for achieving those goals. We're so laser-focused on the goals that we don't pay nearly enough attention to what it takes to complete them. So when the team is falling short of meeting its big goals, it's hard to know whether the strategy is wrong or just poorly executed, and if that's the case, how much of it has to do with the team not performing to its full potential? In the resulting uncertainty, we are left to guess at how to address the failure.

UConn Women's Basketball

If you've read either of my first two books, you know I am fascinated by coach Geno Auriemma and UConn Women's basketball. The more I study how they built the most dominant program in college sports (men or women), the more I learn, and the more instructive I believe it can be for all of us as leaders, whether it's in sports or business.

As the freshmen who join the team will tell you, they revere the players who came before them and the winning tradition they created. Since 1995, this tradition includes eleven national championships, appearances in every Final Four since 2008, and the longest winning streak in NCAA Division 1 history at 111 games. The players understand that winning takes a commitment to getting better every day, on and off the court.

If practice makes perfect (or at least excellent), then the better the practices, the more likely the team will play to its potential. What I love about UConn is that the players don't go to practice every day with the goal of winning a national championship. They go to practice to help each other get just a little bit better than they were the day before, with the hope that they improve again, the day after. National championships are not the goal; they are the reward for the daily discipline required to be the best players and best teammates they can be. They continually put themselves in a position to win it all.

> **National championships are not the goal; they are the reward**

With a meticulous attention to detail, the team focuses on outputs that make winning championships possible. The players and the coaching staff don't measure themselves against the other NCAA Division 1 teams; they set their own standard of excellence. This also raises the standards for everyone else. It's among the reasons there are more top-notch, competitive women's basketball programs than ever before. Tennessee's head coach Pat Summit set the bar for UConn. Just as UConn has done it for more than a dozen other universities who today are playing at a high level, with South Carolina, Stanford, Baylor, Oregon, Notre Dame, and Louisville being among them. For UConn, doing this begins with squeezing every ounce of value out of their time together at practice and putting the players in situations that are often far more difficult than they would experience in a game (I've heard some players describe game days by comparison as "having the day off").

If you can buy into a definition of productivity that focuses on maximizing people, time, and other resources, and improving outputs, with the reward as achieving your goals (whatever they may be), then this could be a game-changer at your organization.

The Relationship between Productivity and Psychological Safety

You can provide all the psychological safety in the world to group members, but they won't stay in the group unless they receive tangible value for themselves and their organizations. This fact is highly instructive for teams as well because outstanding people want to self-identify as part of a team that is performing at a high level and eventually becomes renowned for its commitment to excellence.

Productivity in Groups

When I speak to groups about productivity, I ask them about the quality of the topics they discuss (challenges and opportunities), the dynamics and discipline of their conversations, and the tangible takeaways and eventual outcomes realized for themselves and their organizations. Let's take them one at a time:

Quality of topics. As you may have noticed, when you look at the five factors as a reinforcing loop, you need the right people who are willing to create an environment of psychological safety

> **There is a direct link between psychological safety and what the members are willing to talk about.**

because, without it, members will never raise their most pressing issues. There is a direct link between psychological safety and what the members are willing to talk about. Another condition that affects topic quality is preparedness. Do you remember what it felt like as a student to show up for class if you had not done your homework? The last thing you wanted was for the teacher to call on you and expose you for being unprepared. Unprepared people tend to be uninvolved people. Finally, it comes down to efficacy. Group members are unlikely to ask a burning question unless they are confident that the group will be helpful. Otherwise, what's the point?

Discipline of conversation. Even if the quality of the topics is generally good, they won't stay that way long if there's no discipline around the conversation. Poor discipline can run the gamut from a conversation that meanders endlessly, to one that cuts to the chase so quickly that the group never gets to the heart of the matter, to one that jumps to conclusions too immediately. This dynamic feeds into the efficacy narrative and is detrimental to group productivity. Conversational discipline requires the guiding hand of a servant leader and group members who understand the essential rules of engagement.

Tangible takeaways. In addition to conversational discipline negatively impacting efficacy and confidence, your belief that other members can be helpful will affect your willingness to raise an issue. Why put yourself out there to a group of people who can't help you? The reasons can range from competence to familiarity with the topic at hand to how willing fellow members are to bring their A game. (It's easy to see now why having the right people matters so much.) If people go long enough without receiving any tangible takeaways for themselves or their organization, they'll find another group that provides them.

The Biggest Obstacle (By Far)

The good news is the biggest obstacle to group productivity is the easiest to fix and will have the most significant impact on improvement as well. In early 2017, during a conversation about group productivity, a CEO peer group member (let's call him Jim) admitted that he showed up to his meeting every month less prepared than for any other meeting on his calendar. Jim realized what that meant in real-time as the words were leaving his mouth. He went on to say that he would never consider going to a board meeting, staff meeting, or client meeting as ill-prepared as he is for his peer group session. That admission prompted the other members to think about what Jim was saying, only to jump to the same realization.

Then Jim pointed to one woman and said, "Helen, you always seem prepared for these meetings, noticeably better prepared than the rest of us. How much time do you dedicate to doing that?"

Helen responded, "About fifteen minutes."

The aha moment for everyone in the room was that if they all just did what Helen does, and did it before every meeting, it would exponentially improve the group's productivity and efficacy.

Whenever I follow up on that point with other groups, it's been very much the case. What's more, I've shared the essential aspects of this example with every group I've worked with since that 2017 meeting. Interestingly, I've found lack of preparedness to be a pervasive problem.

So why do CEOs tend not to prepare for their group meetings? Part of it is the "I got this" syndrome. In their minds, they understand themselves and their companies well enough to handle or deflect any question that may come their way without anyone noticing. There's also an unwillingness to accept the fact that bringing their A game to every meeting really matters to the other members. They know how much it means for their other meetings, in large part, because it's consequential in a way that it's not with a peer group. Finally, peer groups aren't for spectators. If the members bring their B and C games and don't bring their best selves, it will be a B or C meeting. When you look at some of the stumbling blocks for a group, it comes down to preparation and perspective: a lack of preparation and the attitude that, in the scheme of things, there are no consequences for not preparing.

I've found lack of preparedness to be a pervasive problem.

That said, I've never had a member who identified as being well-prepared say that it took any longer than the fifteen minutes Helen described. It would appear to be a small investment for a big reward.

WHY ASKING GREAT QUESTIONS CHANGES EVERYTHING

Another benefit of being prepared and engaged is that you ask informed questions. If you want to improve, you should continually be asking yourselves questions about how to make that possible. One question leads to another more detailed question. The more questions asked, the more opportunity for learning and discovery. Sometimes, it's about getting to the answer, while frequently, it's just figuring out whether you're asking the right questions. The right answer to the wrong question will lead you down the wrong path more often than not.

In many mastermind groups, there is a process for bringing a complicated topic for discussion with the members. At Vistage Worldwide, the framework for many of these conversations is called issue processing. Vistage developed this model decades ago, and it's still practiced in one form or another in mastermind groups throughout the world.

Issue processing begins with a member (we'll call her Linda) providing a succinct description of the topic (challenge or opportunity), following with why it is important, actions taken to date, and framing a specific question to ask her fellow members. Members are then invited to ask clarifying questions. The genius of the process lies here. Experienced members understand that the questions they ask at this early stage are more about assessing Linda's specific question to the group. It's the time when members can determine whether Linda has identified the source of the problem or just a symptom. High-performing groups demonstrate a patient and a sophisticated understanding of this part of the process and avoid using it to jump to conclusions before they understand the complete picture.

Based on my experience, the initial ask to the group is adjusted anywhere from 80% to 90 percent of the time. If Linda asked about adding to her client roster, but the group discerned that she is trying to grow her overall business, then those are two very different conversations. Adding clients and what it takes to do that is quite different from an approach that may involve adding clients, driving organic growth, and exploring new income streams. If it is determined Linda needs to restate her question (ask of the group), then she would do it at this time, sparking another round of questioning aimed more squarely at the newly specified goal.

> **Imagine taking the opportunity to climb another person's ladder to check out their view**

After completing this segment, members will share their experiences (and provide direct advice if Linda asks for it). After taking it all in, Linda would reflect for a moment, share what resonated with her, and declare what actions she plans to take based on hearing all the perspectives offered during the issue processing exchange.

The magic of this process lives in the quality of the questions and in a member's willingness to listen to other points of view. In the introduction, you saw how the ladder of inference limits the way we see the world.

Imagine taking the opportunity to climb another person's ladder to check out their view. In chapter 2, the pitch team that won the GTECH business turned a get-acquainted interview into a forum to close a deal, all because we asked better questions than our competitors. When we're willing to climb another ladder, focus on questions rather than answers, and do so out of a relentless commitment to helping yourself, your teammates, and your team improve, you start achieving what most people call abundance.

How Groups Serve as Practice Fields for Teams

Does practice make perfect? Probably not. Perfection is a pretty high bar, but most people would agree that practice can improve game-day performance, for individuals and teams alike. Most of us have first-hand knowledge that this is true. Whether you grew up playing a musical instrument or a team sport, you likely practiced your skills for hours on end to learn and improve so that when you performed in a concert or played a game, you were ready to be at your best. The most exceptional musicians and most skilled athletes in the world continue to practice all the time to stay in top form. So it raises the question that if practice makes perfect (or at least better), then why do we do so little of it in business?

Good versus Great

If you Google "practice in business," you'll find pages of links on best practices in business. Search for practice in golf, and you'll discover thousands of links that address how to practice your golf game. It's a simple but telling illustration of how little emphasis we place on practicing in business. It may merely be a by-product of the Jim Collins's adage, "Good is the enemy of great."[40] He explains it by saying that because we have good schools, we don't have great schools. We don't have great government because we have good government. The problem here isn't so much about settling for good; it's about believing that good is good enough: hardly an attitude that's likely to result in world-class performance.

BUILDING SKILL THROUGH PRACTICE

As CEOs think about competing and thriving on the global stage in the next decade, they'd be wise to ask every one of their employees to watch the Olympic Games (now scheduled for 2021). Watching the games, one becomes acquainted with the world's best athletes who, with countless hours of practice, have honed their skills to near-perfection. Ask yourself how a gymnast does what she does on a four-inch beam or how a winning crew team achieves a level of alignment that most companies only dream of. It's through practice: lots of it.

In *The Fifth Discipline: The Art and Practice of the Learning Organization*, Peter Senge wrote about the importance of creating practice fields in business.[41] Take a moment and think about whether you create practice fields in your company. Peer advisory groups? Live simulations? Retreats? Gaming? No one wins an Olympic medal for just being good. It's not likely that your business will thrive on the global stage over the next ten years for just being good, either. Think about how you conduct practice to make your company the best.

PRODUCTIVITY IN TEAMS

Again, if we imagine productivity in terms of outputs as well as outcomes, it helps us reimagine how we can work together more effectively. How many times have you heard someone complain that their company's team is understaffed? The organization may be understaffed, but it's also quite possible that the team is not maximizing all the efficiencies and synergies available to them. Productivity in teams comes down to the following:

Teammates. Having the right people on the team who are committed to bringing their A games and being good teammates is essential to team success. Consider my team from Wooding & Housley that pitched the GTECH business. Not one or even two of us could have brought all the skills or thinking necessary to winning that account. It took everything that each of us could uniquely contribute to the task at hand. Being good teammates wasn't just done out of courtesy and friendship; it was a necessity. It's about truly embracing the axiom, "None of us is as smart as all of us." It's that anything is possible as long as no one cares who gets the credit, and no matter what happens, the team will either celebrate or mourn without assigning credit or blame. We win together and lose together. Simple as that.

Processes. How team members work together is the difference between having great players and having a great team. It starts with establishing the rules of engagement, when possible through a written charter; each team member should understand how the team plans to work together. Bruce Tuckman's construct of forming, storming, norming, and performing has stood the test of time, yet used so infrequently. The forming stage is the essential step; it sets the tone for how the team will work going forward. Think about these processes during the forming stage:

- Meetings (how often will you have them and what are they designed to accomplish?).
- Calendaring (what's the protocol for scheduling people in a manner that doesn't highjack their time from other important commitments?).
- Virtual work (what tools and resources will allow for the best possible real-time communication and transparency? This is an all-important skill that was forced upon organizational leaders in 2020.

Milestones. The loftiest goals for most teams in sports or business typically take time. Keeping a team engaged and inspired by showing them their continued progress or celebrating milestones along the way can be essential to sustaining individual and team excellence throughout the process.

Results. People love to self-identify with winning teams. Fans will happily sport a football jersey from their hometown team but feel much better after the team wins a Super Bowl. Being from New England, I have lots of experience with this. I don't say that to gloat at all. I use the Patriots to illustrate what it feels like at both ends of the spectrum. I'm sixty years old, so when I was growing up, the Patriots couldn't buy a win, let alone compete for a Super Bowl. Not only did you not find a whole lot of people sporting Patriots garb, I had neighbors who proudly wore New

York Giants apparel (sacrilegious as that sounds). Today's New England Patriots bear no example to the team I knew growing up. I bet Patriots merchandise sales are up just a bit since the 1960s, '70s, and early '80s.

Making the Connection Between Groups and Teams

As defined previously, groups convene to help individual members achieve their goals. Teams work together toward achieving a collective goal or creating a common work product. That said, sometimes groups are required to work as teams. For example, in a graduate school cohort, class members help each other learn more effectively so that each class member can receive the best possible individual grade. However, they may be asked to work as a team by collaborating to write a single paper or complete a video project they are graded collectively on. Teams may be assembled to achieve a common goal or work product, but in the process, they will work together in groups to hone their individual skills, thus making them better individual contributors to the team.

In sales teams, for example, those who are excellent at prospecting, closing, or explaining a product or service in a particularly compelling way can help other salespeople improve. Sales teams who believe in abundance and who work together to make the pie bigger will be stronger than sales teams who come from a place of scarcity, concerned only with their individual performance, assuming a finite pie, and who only care about fighting for their slice.

Meetings

It's time to shake things up a bit. Most staff meetings follow an all-too-familiar agenda: 1) The leader of the meeting makes a few announcements. 2) Meeting participants take turns giving reports about what's happening in their department. 3) The meeting ends with a feeling of faux satisfaction and the belief that everyone is informed and aligned, at least until the next meeting. Does this sound like your weekly staff meeting? If it does, then let's look at an alternative.

During numerous conversations with former Vistage CEO Rafael Pastor, he often spoke about the idea of running a staff meeting similar to that of a peer advisory group. With that in mind, let me propose a new agenda for your next meeting:

1. As the leader of the meeting, don't start by covering everything *you* believe is most important. And rather than ask *what* your people are doing, ask *how* they are doing. Create a forum where your employees can share personal milestones and express how they feel personally and professionally. It not only sends a message that you care about the people as opposed to just the work, but also sets the right tone for upcoming conversations. This was among the biggest takeaways for CEOs who were forced to lead virtual teams during the pandemic.
2. Ask someone who's recently attended a conference, read a relevant business book, or enrolled in an outside course to take ten minutes to share what they learned last week. That way, everyone receives value, and it sharpens the employee's presentation skills to boot. (Identify the person before the meeting so she or he is prepared.)
3. Make your announcements, promote dialogue, and then invite individuals to raise issues or challenges that they believe the members could help address. This exercise leverages your breadth of talent, builds trust and camaraderie, and may help your team accomplish something.
4. Close by asking everyone to express in one sentence their top priority for the upcoming week. It provides a point of focus for the employee and benefits the team as well.
5. Adjourn.

Chapter Summary

Consider productivity as covering both outputs and outcomes. There's never been a time in human history when we have to depend on each other more. The good news is that we have the tools and the wherewithal to collaborate with anyone in the world who can contribute to a positive outcome, whether such an outcome pertains to individuals, organizations, or ecosystems. To that end, we have to be willing to check out the view from someone else's ladder by being curious enough to ask questions and secure enough to consider their responses with an open mind and an open heart.

Groups are where teams should practice. It's where they can hone their skills to learn rather than judge and exhibit all the behaviors of psychological safety that make such honest exchanges so fruitful.

What's Next?

Chapter 5 explores what group and team member accountability is all about. Spoiler alert: It's not about accountability to a group leader, coach, or CEO; it's about accountability to other team members and building and sustaining a culture of personal responsibility over the long haul.

CHAPTER 5
Accountability

> Leadership is getting players to believe in you. If you tell a teammate you're ready to play as tough as you're able to, you'd better go out there and do it. Players will see right through a phony.[42]
> —Larry Bird

During the 1980s, Larry Bird and Magic Johnson's rivalry turned friendship is the quintessential example of how people can make each other and their teams better. Two NBA stars with Midwest roots (playing on different teams on opposite coasts), and who met only twice a year during the regular season, used each other as measuring sticks for greatness. They contributed to team wins in every facet of the game on both ends of the floor and made their respective teammates better in the process.

Magic and Bird checked each other's game stats every night and motivated one another to practice their craft just a little bit harder every day. The fact that they both believed that the power of we begins with me is evident in their example. They knew that a great team started with them. Their mutual respect helped them become better players and more effective team leaders. Bird and Magic each won three league MVP awards, and the Lakers and Celtics combined to win eight NBA Championships during that era.

What distinguishes these teams for me (my bias as a lifelong Celtics fan notwithstanding) is how they won. Both squads had star players who sported an incredible worth ethic and commitment to excellence, driven by their coaches and their leaders: Magic and Bird. The Lakers and the Celtics played a brand of team basketball that, from my perspective, set a high-water mark that still exists today. If you're a basketball fan, I invite you to enjoy the countless Celtics-Lakers YouTube videos from that era. They speak for themselves. Even if you're not a fan or know nothing about the sport, it's difficult to miss the beauty of their level of teamwork.

> **Their mutual respect helped them become better players and more effective team leaders**

On a final note, the fans played a big part here as well. As you know, customers are among the ultimate judges of effort and commitment to excellence for companies. Magic, Bird, the Lakers, and the Celtics realized they were always accountable to their fans. Celtics fans loved their team as much as they despised the Lakers, and vice versa. I suspect the bicoastal rivalry among fans made them better too. There is one particular example from 1982 that I'll never forget.

The Celtics were hosting the Philadelphia 76ers at Boston Garden for Game 7 of the Eastern Conference Finals. Boston and Philly were bitter rivals, to say the least. Boston lost that game at home, 120–106. What makes it memorable, though, was not that it was only the second time the Celtics ever lost a Game 7 at home; it was what happened before the final buzzer. When it was evident that the game was out of reach, the sold-out Garden crowd began chanting, "Beat LA! Beat LA," the team the 76ers would meet in the NBA Finals. I can only imagine what that must have been like for the 76ers players to be cheered by Boston fans at the end of a Game 7 Celtics loss. Of course, Boston fans were sending a message to the West Coast: As much as we loath Philly, we hate the Lakers even more! This event would set the stage for the bitter 1984 NBA Championship series, when Boston and LA would play for the championship for the first time in that incredible decade.

Personal Experience

You may find it helpful to pause for a moment and reflect on the people in your life who pushed you to be better. These people could have been people you admired from afar, like Magic and Bird, or coworkers you competed with. We know about the relationship between Magic and Bird, but most observers are not as familiar with Larry Bird's relationship with his teammate, Dennis Johnson. Bird regarded Johnson as the best teammate he ever had. They helped each other advance their understanding of the game and enjoyed an on-court chemistry that leveraged their great basketball minds.

I'm not making any qualitative comparisons to Magic and Bird here, but I would regard Paul Sabattus, who was a client of mine for many years and remains a friend today, as my Magic. This fact is especially fitting since he was a Lakers fan. I admired Paul's presence and creativity. He pushed me to be a better professional, and we had a great deal of fun doing it. My Dennis Johnson* was Marty Lynch. He was among the best people I've ever worked with. Marty was a true student of his craft, always willing to explore what's next and implement it, often before the CEO was ready to do so. He was on the bleeding edge. I respected him for it, and I have done my best to stay future-focused because of his influence. (*Note: I'm sure Marty is reading this and thinking, "Wait a minute; I'm the Larry Bird here." To which I would say to Marty, "You can be Larry when you write your book!")

All kidding aside, the point here is that peer influence, peer pressure, peer modeling, or whatever else you want to call it, is a powerful force in our lives. Left to our own devices, most of us will only go so far.

> **Great teammates have shared goals and shared values, and they hold themselves accountable for both.**

We need people who can help us be our best selves and, by doing so, make us more effective contributors to any team. Great teammates have shared goals and shared values, and they hold themselves accountable for both.

ACCOUNTABILITY AND VALUES

In the late 1990s, United Way produced a video that cleverly poked fun at itself, while also making an important point. The scene was an elementary school classroom where a student brought her dad (a United

Way exec) to talk about what he does for a living. As Dad launches into his "United Way jargon," the kids quickly look bored. The daughter immediately senses the problem, stands up, and clarifies his work for everyone by exclaiming, "He helps people!" Fortunately, Dad picked up on the cue and began engaging the class. The boredom quickly gave way to comprehension and smiles.

I couldn't help thinking of that story after Vistage chair John Younker responded to a blog post I had written titled "What Core Values Drive Your Peer Advisory Group?" In his comment, he shared the unifying principles that guided the Vistage group he led in Texas at the time. John and his group cut to the core with the same elegant simplicity that the daughter of the United Way exec articulated in her classroom. For them, it's about being there for one another. Saying it is one thing; delivering on it is quite another. John and his group do so in two important ways:[43]

1. They give their statement meaning through a code of conduct that guides the specific behaviors of the group members. The group's code is as follows:

   Candor. We will be open and candid with one another; we will say what we are thinking.

   Care. We have permission to confront another member caringly, even when doing so makes that member feel uncomfortable.

   Openness. If we feel a member is holding back and not being open and candid with us, we will confront that member.

   Trust. We trust that we can trust in one another; we can count on each other to honor the confidentiality agreement we all signed when we joined the group.

   Confidentiality. We will inform the whole group whenever we feel there has been a violation of a rule; it will be a group issue to address and resolve.

Supportive. We are encouraged to ask for support and assistance when we feel we need it at any time, even between the times of our monthly meetings.

Respect. We will show respect to one another and our commitment to being present and on time at our meetings.

2. To ensure that their unifying principles and accompanying code of conduct are more than just words, the group holds a retreat at the end of each year, where they evaluate their performance and effectiveness, based primarily on their code. After the retreat, the members draft a memorandum to John, identifying how they can improve over the following year, and they hold themselves accountable for delivering on their recommendations.

John's group walks the talk by being there for one another in word and deed. It's what makes for a successful group, and it's among the reasons John and his members find the peer advisory experience so valuable.

It's worth noting that every one of these conduct codes and behaviors applies to what it takes to ensure psychological safety. When you look at codes of conduct or rules of the road for most groups, they almost always do. When I ask members to rate their member-to-member accountability, it almost always matches what they rated as their ability to leverage their safe and confidential environment. This finding means that while members may rate their psychological safety as a 9.5 or 10, they almost always rate their ability to truly leverage that environment far less generously; on average, it's closer to 6.5. So if group members rate themselves a 6.5 on psychological safety, it's a good bet that they'll use the same number (or lower) to rate their member-to-member accountability. The alignment is neither a coincidence nor an accident. If you can't truly leverage psychological safety, you will never feel comfortable enough to challenge each or hold each other to account in any serious manner.

> *John's group walks the talk by being there for one another in word and deed.*

Accountability as Personal Responsibility

If you're part of a team and think that the success of the team begins with you (like Magic and Bird), then you've taken a first step to accepting the personal responsibility you should ask of yourself and expect from others. Coaches and peers can push you, but you have to want to be great. You also need to be the kind of person who is willing to help others perform to their potential. To do that requires commitment. It's not something others should hold you accountable for, so much as something you accept as your responsibility to yourself and others.

> **Coaches and peers can push you, but you have to want to be great.**

My bent toward thinking about accountability in personal responsibility terms, the dictionary notwithstanding, comes from several sources. I was initially intrigued by the words of Pasi Sahlberg, a professor and the former director-general of the Centre for International Mobility and Cooperation (CIMO) in Finland. Professor Sahlberg once stated that there was no direct translation for the word *accountability* in the Finnish language.[44] He said that accountability is what's left after someone's sense of personal responsibility gives way. After first reading this, it forced me to evaluate how much of it may be semantics or a cleverly turned phrase versus something more substantive.

The more I listened to CEOs share their focus on holding people accountable, the more I noticed how it almost always put their employees on the defensive. It created a dynamic that looked more like two people sitting on opposite sides as opposed to being on the same side. As a result, employees did not own their performance so much as leaders were imposing it on them. Even for employees who hit their goals, their head may be in it, but their heart is not, and certainly not for the long term.

Finally, I found that people who don't accept personal responsibility for their work and own their goals tend to believe that they don't matter much. These people can't imagine that bringing their A games every day and contributing to the team with their very best could make any kind of a real difference. Over time, they become accustomed to coasting by and believing that as long as they do work that is reasonably acceptable, they can hang on without fear of repercussion or damaging the team or the organization. This mindset is a false narrative, and it plays out among CEO group members and employees alike.

Personal Responsibility and the CEO

About a year ago, I was leading my Harnessing Peer Advantage to Your Advantage workshop for a group of CEOs in the Midwest. We were talking about accountability and personal responsibility. We covered it in three categories, which I'll review in greater detail shortly. The first category discussed was values and behaviors. The group members shared the common challenge of being the chief decision-makers at their companies. They also accept personal responsibility for modeling behaviors based on the values they have agreed are necessary for being a valuable contributor to the group. Typical among such values is commitment, often defined by group members themselves as a combination of being prepared for the meeting, attending every session, and being truly present during the time they spend together.

Next is follow-up on action items. When one member engages the group to help address an upcoming challenge, other members will share their personal experiences and, by doing so, provide insights and perspectives. The member processes the dialogue and typically reaches her own conclusion regarding the next steps. She agrees to follow up with the group on her progress. This follow-up is also important because of the learning opportunities that come from such conversations.

Finally, there is an expectation that members will challenge one another to "do what they said they would do" (DWTSTWD). The group members are not telling the member what to do, only asking that she come to her own conclusion and act in a fashion that will help her achieve what she wants for herself. This ownership is one of the key differences between the dynamic of a peer group and hiring a consultant. Rather than being told what to do (not that we don't need that sometimes), the CEO owns the solution, and because of that, we've learned that owning it makes it far more likely it will be implemented successfully.

Among these three categories, you would think the least controversial conversation would be about attendance as an essential behavior. Yet, it was, and in a rather dramatic way.

Attendance

Interestingly enough, there was a gentleman in the room (I'll call him Richard) who had less-than-stellar attendance when it came to his monthly group meeting. I noticed that the more I talked about the importance of being there every month, the more it appeared to annoy him. Evidently, the conversation went on too long for his liking, so he let everyone know in uncertain terms that he's the member and pays his dues, so if he chooses not to attend, then that's his prerogative. He threw down the gauntlet and said, "If I don't show up to the meetings, it's my loss, no one else's."

He looked up at me in front of the room as if to say, "Okay; now what?" What he didn't realize was by telling everyone that when he can't make the meeting, he is the only one who loses, it gave me an opening. I waited a second or two and directed a question to one of the other members.

I asked, "Would you mind taking one minute to tell the group what's missing from the conversation when Richard is not here?" I asked a second member and then a third. They all spoke directly to Richard and explained what was lost from the conversation when he wasn't in attendance. They told him how he brings a perspective that no other member provides and that his presence in the room matters a great deal.

I turned back to Richard to find him welling up with tears. Richard knew full well how much he mattered as the CEO back at his organization, but he had no idea what his participation meant to his fellow members.

> **You can't remove an instrument and expect the ensemble to produce the same sound. Everybody matters.**

I assured Richard that I didn't do that to show him up. I looked at the group and said, "The fact is, I could have asked the same question about any one of you and received a similar response. Think of it as a jazz ensemble. You can't remove an instrument and expect the ensemble to produce the same sound. Everybody matters."

Richard turned to his members and said he had no idea how much his poor attendance was impacting the people in the room. He went on to vow that he would do his best never to miss another meeting.

Values and Adding Value

While the diversity of the group members is enormously important to providing a broad range of perspectives to the group, what the members believe when it comes to what it takes to be a strong contributor is equally important. When I reflected on how CEO groups in America and the UK think about diversity and shared values, I found that they value both. Still, US CEOs tend to place a greater emphasis on diversity, while UK CEOs showed a bent toward shared values.

American CEOs often participate in groups with other CEOs who lead companies outside their industry sectors. This dynamic helps avoid having competitors in the room, and it provides these leaders with a window into how things are done elsewhere. It's how they discover practices that are unheard of in their industry but are commonplace elsewhere and could work for them as well. They seek out not only CEOs from different industries but also those who have specific strengths such as marketing, finance, legal, and human resources. Diversity also speaks to age, gender, race, and ethnicity. Anyone can participate in the group and provide a lens on a situation that most individual members don't see.

UK CEOs, participating in the same multi-industry sector groups, place a big premium on diversity as well. Still, when asked about adding members to their group who could add value, their first inclination is to talk about recruits in terms of shared values. They spoke of prospective members as being willing to be committed, being vulnerable, being there to learn rather than judge others, and being able to leave their egos at the door. They believed that having someone who checked off the box as being from a different industry or having different skill sets didn't necessarily translate into their adding value. Unless they could "chin the bar" on shared values, they would never add value.

Show Up, Step Up, Follow Up

If you're a peer advisory group member and want your group to perform at an even higher level, understand that it all starts with you. Being a more valuable group member is the first step to building an even higher performing group. As Jim Kouzes and Barry Posner so famously outlined in their five exemplary leadership practices, it's up to you to "Model the Way."[45] You may not be the leader of your group, but you can always be a leader in your group.

After four years of helping new and experienced peer advisory groups squeeze the most value out of their time together, two findings consistently emerged. First, the strength of the overall group rests in the hands of its members. To be high-performing, each individual needs to be all in. Second, there are three things members can do to immediately up their game to everyone's advantage: Show up. Step up. Follow up.

Show up. If you believe that 80 percent of life is about showing up, then understand that to be an outstanding member, it's that and then some. If you (and your fellow members) don't attend meetings consistently, the group will never realize its true potential. As you know, I use the five factors for high-performing peer groups described in *The Power of Peers* to help groups assess their current performance against what they believe to be ideal. These factors include:

1. all the right people in the room
2. a safe and confidential environment
3. valuable interactions that provide meaningful and actionable takeaways
4. a culture of member-to-member accountability
5. a servant leader who serves as the steward of the first four factors

Every time you don't attend a meeting, it's not just a loss for you; you're sabotaging the group's ability to perform at its best. Life happens, but being a great member starts with being there.

Step up. Since you're going to the meeting, you might as well bring your A game. This effort starts with being prepared. To review, CEOs, small business owners, and key executives alike have admitted to me countless times that they are less prepared for their group meetings than any other meeting on their calendar. For those who do prepare, it's evident to the other members, and best of all, it's easy. I haven't had one prepared member tell me that it takes any more than fifteen minutes to get ready for a group meeting. The better prepared you are, the more engaged you'll be. The more involved everyone is, the better your group will perform.

Follow up. Let's say you ask for assistance from your group to either assess a potential opportunity or address a tough challenge. With the group's help, you decide how you will proceed. Be sure to follow up with the group at the next meeting (and after that, as necessary). Letting your members know what you've done serves as an expression of gratitude for the time they spent helping you; it contributes to a positive culture of member-to-member accountability and becomes an invaluable learning opportunity for everyone. The learning happens when everyone finds out about what worked and what didn't work: valuable information that eventually becomes a critical part of a group's ever-changing DNA.

THE POWER OF WE BEGINS WITH ME

I remember the workshop I'm about to describe for two reasons. It involved one of the most robust conversations among members I have ever witnessed in a group. The members crawled inside each of the five factors with enthusiasm and relentless depth. The more they talked, the more they learned about themselves, and the more they enjoyed doing so.

At the very end of the meeting, one of the members (I'll call him Phil) stood up and pulled an envelope out of his pocket. In it was a letter he had written to the leader of the group, explaining in great detail how the group was not providing him value, and as a result, he was leaving the group. After telling us what was in the letter, he proceeded to tear it up.

He said, "I've spent the last three hours talking with you all and realizing that the reason I'm not getting value is not because of you all; it's because of me. I don't want to leave the group. I owe you all an apology for not living up to my responsibilities as a good member. That changes starting today. From this day forward, I'll do everything in my power to be the best member I can be, and if you ever see me slacking off, someone needs to kick me in the butt."

I can only imagine what Phil was going through during the workshop. Think about it. Here we are engaging in a three-hour exercise about how to improve a group he had already decided to leave. To his credit, he willingly participated in the morning conversations from the start and never displayed any disinterest or negativity. What's more, even if the workshop inspired a change of heart, most people might have just kept the letter in their pocket and never said a word. Sharing the message with his members was his way of hitting the reset button. He stated that from now on, he'd bring his A game, and by the power of his example, he expected others to do the same.

Chapter Summary

Larry Bird and Magic Johnson, whose relationship was the subject of an HBO documentary and a Broadway play, have a great deal to teach us. Their lesson is about having people in our lives who light the fire within us to achieve a level of excellence that would otherwise be unattainable. Leaders bring their very best to every team situation and, in the process, set an example and work with everyone on the team to realize their full potential; they are team leaders of the highest order. It's about accepting responsibility for accountability, and when team members do that for one another, their team is an indomitable force. Driven by shared values and behaviors, the three keys to any team success are showing up, stepping up, and following up. The power of we begins with you.

> **Sharing the message with his members was his way of hitting the reset button.**

What's Next?

What does excellent group and team leadership look like, and how will you prepare to lead? I'll share a few stories, using both negative and positive examples, along with offering some ideas about how leadership can make a difference for any group or team. As you read the stories in the next chapter, ask yourself whether your current leadership style is closer to Roy or Joe. Regardless of your response, how will you lead your team in the future?

CHAPTER 6
Leadership

> If I have seen further, it is by standing on the shoulders of giants.[46]
> —Isaac Newton

EVERYBODY I'VE EVER MET HAS HAD A BOSS WHO SERVED AS THEIR personal example of how *not* to lead people. Here's one of mine. After my graduation from Jacksonville University in April 1983, there was roughly a six-month gap between then and when I was supposed to start a position with US Senator Paul Tsongas's re-election campaign. With no money and no car, I accepted a job that would provide me both: it was a sales position at a local Ford dealership where I could earn a decent living and, after a thirty-day probationary period, drive a brand-new car.

To set the leadership stage, there was the owner, the general manager, and the sales manager. The owner was pretty much irrelevant, at least in terms of any direct contact with the sales team. The general manager's name was John, a well-dressed Bob Newhart figure, both in terms of his understated demeanor and his sense of humor. Roy, the sales manager, was a chain-smoking tyrant. The duo was textbook good cop, bad cop. The dynamic was similar to what I remembered from junior high school, with the ambassador-like principal who everyone loved and the badass assistant principal who everybody feared.

At the dealership, Roy was our assistant principal, so to speak. To paint a picture, he rode everyone hard, all the time. If he sensed a hint of inactivity in your eyes, he would literally throw a phonebook at you and tell you to call twenty landscapers and sell them a truck. Keep in mind, Roy was also the person who had to get involved before any customer left the building. One of my many stories of Roy not only killing a deal, but mentally scarring the participating parties for life, involved a woman who came in to buy her first new car. She spent months visiting dealerships and was doing her best to get a great deal on a new Ford Escort. When she balked at the price I offered her, I had no choice but to get Roy involved, in an effort to give it one last try.

> **The duo was textbook good cop, bad cop.**

Roy sat next to me at my desk and politely asked the woman how he could help her. She asked him to give her a bottom-line price for the car she wanted. When he would not, she proceeded to tell us that other dealerships had no problem doing so at all. It was at that point that she pulled about a dozen business cards out of her purse and then flipped them over to show the price each dealer had offered. They were laid out all across the desk. He looked at her, looked at me, and looked at her again. I knew what was coming, but his vehemence surprised me.

Roy screamed, "Are you trying to buy a car or wallpaper your _____ bathroom? Get the _____ out of here."

He got up and left; the two of us sat there for a moment, and then I said, "Okay, thanks for coming by."

And she left forever, as you might imagine. Was this woman ever going to buy a car from us? Probably not. It does, however, give you a window into Roy's rather unique approach to leadership and the transactional nature of how he viewed the world.

A Thank You Note, Crayon, and Hot Wheels

Roy had a bit of a reputation for getting into accidents with the company cars he drove. One morning, his Crown Victoria arrived at the dealership via tow truck. Roy's story was that a two-and-a-half-year-old kid had crawled out into the middle of the street, and to avoid hitting the child, he swerved and crashed into a tree. Of course, from everybody's perspective, the story was suspect, not the least of which was the specificity of the child's age: not two years old, not three, but two-and-a-half. After having already heard this tall tale about an hour earlier, I was standing next to a colleague watching the car get hauled in, and for whatever reason, I said, "Hey, I'm going to give Roy a hard time about the accident and this whole crazy story."

My colleague skeptically replied, "Really? I look forward to seeing that." He had a point. Any direct mention of this would have been professional death for me. There had to be another way.

John, the general manager, led a meeting every Monday morning where he updated us on new inventory, talked about incentive programs, and frequently shared letters from satisfied customers. Everyone in sales, including Roy, attended. Before the next Monday morning meeting began, I handed John a letter in a sealed envelope. I had written the letter using a crayon with my non-dominant hand and explained to John that it was from the two-and-a-half-year-old kid, thanking Roy for not hitting him with his car. Also enclosed in the envelope was a blue Crown Victoria Hot Wheels car so that Roy would have something to use while his vehicle was being fixed.

Given John's dry sense of humor, it's hard to imagine a better person to have read the letter to the team, and he was a more-than-willing accomplice to the prank. Before closing the meeting, he announced receipt of the letter, read it aloud, and passed it around to everyone at the table. John was impressed at the kid's letter-writing skills and also applauded his forgiving disposition and generosity. To this day, I've never seen a group of grown men so overcome with tears of laughter, nor did I ever witness Roy's face glean such a color red.

Roy spent the rest of the day trying to find out who did it. After lunch, he walked up to me and said, "I know you did it, you ____." Amused, but feeling he still had to punish me for what I did in some way, he made me move about a dozen cars to different locations in the parking lot in the blazing heat. For me, it as well worth it.

Leadership and Teams

Besides offering a bit of comic relief, I share this story from my car dealership days with you for several reasons. Roy's leadership style wasn't just command-and-control; it was unapologetically transactional. I suppose if you needed someone to come in and turn things around in the short term (like a week or two), Roy would undoubtedly light a fire under a team and make it happen. The other dynamic at work here is that Roy was not a part of the team; he was apart from it. It wasn't until decades later that I understood the significance of this. I just knew there had to be a better way to lead, for employees and customers alike.

> Roy's leadership style wasn't just command-and-control; it was unapologetically transactional.

Fast-forward to my graduate school experience at Seton Hall University, where I was introduced to *The Leadership Challenge* by Jim Kouzes and Barry Posner. This book is currently in its sixth edition and has been translated into twenty-two languages to date. It's where I first read about the distinction between lighting a fire under someone and lighting the fire within,[47] which speaks to the difference between motivation and inspiration. In Roy's world, salespeople would work harder to avoid being hit by a phonebook. One might call that motivating, but it's hardly inspiring.

Are Leaders Part of the Team or Apart from It?

Over the years, I have asked many leaders, "Do you consider yourself a part of the team, or do you think of yourself as apart from it?" Some leaders say they are part of the team; others see themselves as separate from the team, while many were not quite sure what I was asking. While some leaders like to consider themselves part of the team, they struggle with the concept, both intellectually and in practice. In large part, it's because they believe they are there to direct, coach, and provide support, but they're not really on the team.

Here's what a leader being part of the team looks like: Years ago, while working at Mullen (today MullenLowe), I participated in a new business pitch to a major prospective client in New York. Agency CEO Joe Grimaldi closed the presentation by stating to the prospect, "You won't come across another agency who will care more than Mullen about your business and your success." I had been at the agency just long enough to want to stand up in that moment and say, "He's right, you know." I had worked for several agencies over the years, and it was the first time in my life I had ever heard those words delivered by a CEO with such conviction and sincerity, and I knew the agency actually had the culture to back it up.

For starters, Mullen's CEO was part of the presentation team from the get-go. Joe Grimaldi didn't just show up on game day. His presence at the meeting was a clear demonstration to the prospective client that its business mattered to the agency. Grimaldi later showed us that our team was essential to him, too. After the presentation, he received an urgent call that took him out of the room as we were packing up before flying back to Boston. None of us gave it a second thought until we got home that night. Before going to bed, I checked my email and discovered a note he sent to everyone on the team, apologizing for being pulled away. He said that he failed us in his role as chief encouragement officer but went on to applaud everyone's collective effort and state that regardless of the outcome, we had every reason to celebrate the great work we did together.

> **Stage 5 is the "Life is Great" culture. This culture depicts the rarified air where organizations set their own standard of excellence.**

Grimaldi's words during the presentation and to the team that night, spoke to the culture that he, executive creative director Edward Boches, and others had built over many years. While I was there, the leaders lived it, modeled it, and inspired it in everyone at the agency. (Mullen won the business, by the way.)

THE POWER OF THE LEADERSHIP TRIAD

Years later, in 2012, I became acquainted with a groundbreaking book titled *Tribal Leadership* and had the good fortune to spend time with one of its coauthors, Dave Logan. A central theme of the narrative is its five stages of culture, which the authors ascribed (by percentage) to companies that live these cultures every day. The results were sobering and instructive when it comes to the value of being part of the team.

Stage 1 is the "Life Sucks" culture. As you might imagine, this creates a work environment that resembles a prison gang more than a place of employment. Based on their research, the authors said that roughly 2 percent of companies fall into this toxic category. Stage 2 is the "My Life Sucks" culture. The authors claim that 25 percent of companies have people who fundamentally do just enough work to keep from being fired. These employees say, "Your life may be fine, but mine, not so much." They can't wait for their workday to end, and their weekend plans take precedence over anything that might involve bringing their A game to the job. Stage 3 is the "I'm Great (You're Not)" environment, found in 49 percent of companies. This culture features command-and-control leaders, who would certainly be categorized as operating apart from their teams as opposed to a part of them. Stage 4 is the "We're Great" culture, in which organizations are passionate about beating their competitors and being the top dog, typically as it relates to their industry sector. Stage 5 is the "Life is Great" culture. This culture depicts the rarified air where organizations set their own standard of excellence. According to Logan, nobody lives in that stage all the time. Yet I would suggest Mullen indeed visits Stage 5 frequently, and the University of Connecticut women's basketball team is as close as it gets to establishing permanent residence there.[48]

During our research for *The Power of Peers*, we found that when examining high-performing groups and teams, the high performers had leaders who were a part of a group or team, rather than apart from it. Figure 11 paints a picture.

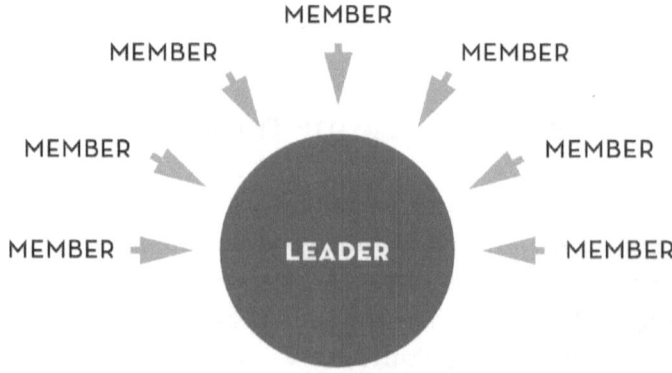

Figure 11. Stage 3: "I'm Great (You're Not)"

Note the relationship between the leader and the team members as well as the relationship the members have with one another. You see lots of dyad relationships with the leader and no visual team dynamic at all. This is what being apart from the team looks like. That's how so many companies are run, but it hardly promotes much in the way of true teamwork.

Figure 12 was developed in cooperation with Dave Logan during the writing of *The Power of Peers*.

Figure 12. The leadership triad

In this model, the leader, the group/team member, and the group/team itself are connected and realize they all have a role in ensuring their success. While the word "Results" sits in the middle of the triad, you could replace that with whatever outcome you like, including a positive culture, productivity, alignment, engagement, and so on. It's not about a team trying to achieve results for the leader or team members looking to the leader as a single source of inspiration. Every member of the triad enjoys a shared responsibility for achieving excellence.

WHY SOME LEADERS HAVE TROUBLE WITH BEING PART OF THE TEAM

When I ask leaders if they believe they are a part of the team or not, most of them hedge for a moment and then respond, "No." They see their role as separate and in many cases don't always want to be viewed as part of their team because of how they perceive their job as the leader. I often hear comparisons between the coach on a sports team, who they would argue is not one of the team members. This is where the definition of *team* is subject to debate. Just because coaches don't take the field with the players doesn't mean they are not a part of the team. It's the whole team that makes winning possible, not just the players.

In mastermind groups, depending on the organization running them, groups can be led by Chairs (Vistage) or members trained as facilitators (YPO). In both cases, these leaders are a part of their groups; they don't sit apart from them. This is essential, because as part of the group, they participate and model certain behaviors to members that make the entire group (and their leadership of the group) far more effective. They deliver in their leadership role as pictured in the drawing of the triad yet also demonstrate, through their active participation, the same level of curiosity, vulnerability, generosity, and courage they expect from everyone around the table. They would never ask a group member to do anything they wouldn't do themselves.

Team members want to know that their leaders are in the fight with them, not looking on from a distance. Teams should be set up so they win or lose as one. They accept the credit and share the blame together. If you want to lead your team and be really effective at it for the long term, make sure you consider yourself part of the team, and be sure your team members realize it as well.

Why Being Part of the Team Mattered During the Pandemic

During the first four months of the pandemic, I participated in numerous conversations with CEOs in their peer groups, who talked enthusiastically about the performance and productivity of teams that were now forced to work from home. Those CEOs who considered themselves part of their teams tended to share a higher level of empathy with their employees, recognizing that such productivity could be short-lived if they didn't attend to the following imminent challenges:

1. **Burnout** – Getting off to a fast start is great, but it's a long race, and maintaining the energy it will require to sustain or even improve upon these high productivity levels will also require coaching employees to take breaks during the day to help with their mental and physical health.
2. **Obscurity** – It can be hard enough for many employees to feel that anyone really sees how hard they are working when they are in the office, let alone while they are at home. Finding ways to let individuals and their teams know that their hard work and accomplishments are visible to their leaders and their peers within the company, beyond their immediate supervisor and fellow teammates, is essential.
3. **Isolation** – As social beings, we can start to feel isolated and alone really quickly – especially if we are living alone. Scheduling regular work meetings and team social gatherings (that can even involve family members when applicable) can help create a sense of connectedness that can be compromised in a virtual work setting.
4. **Insolation** – When we become too insolated, our thinking tends to become even more siloed. It's a tough enough problem when everyone comes to a central office. This is where the work of cross-functional work teams becomes essential. Departmental leaders can deliver an important perspective that can keep employees connected to what's happening in the business as a whole – a view that can be difficult to achieve when employees are heads down working on their particular projects.
5. **Inspiration** – A healthy dose of celebration can serve as an antidote to burnout, obscurity, isolation, and insolation. The more that CEOs can creatively celebrate small wins along the way, the more likely they can keep spirits high. Think of Joe Grimaldi and his role as chief encouragement officer.

When it comes to productivity, CEOs who are part of the team don't take for granted that what they are experiencing at any given time is what they will see long-term. Great leaders serve their employees by being empathetic stewards of the first four factors (people, psychological safety, productivity, accountability) as a part of their teams, not apart from them.

More Leadership Lessons from Leading Groups

To lead a mastermind group effectively, you have to be able to fill the chair. You need the desire, passion, skills, brain, heart, and stomach to handle the awesome responsibility that comes with leading a group of CEOs, small business owners, and senior-level executives. You're a professional facilitator, coach, friend, and confidante who helps leaders manage their lives and their livelihoods. Moreover, just imagine what their work means to the families, employees, vendors, friends, and communities who depend on these leaders.

I have a great deal of respect for anyone who leads these groups successfully. That said, you can imagine my delight when I was invited to join nineteen Vistage Worldwide best practice chairs for dinner several years ago. During dinner, I asked several of them this simple question: What does it take to be an excellent peer advisory group leader? Here's a sample of what I heard:

1. Passion. A great chair has to have a passion for the work.
2. Caring. You have to genuinely care about the welfare of others, on both personal and professional levels.
3. Listening (the attribute I heard most consistently). More listening (understanding), less talking (assuming or prescribing).
4. Managing the energy in the room. A comment directed explicitly at the group experience and the importance of keeping a group focused, productive, and performing to its true potential.
5. Safety. Every member of the group has to feel safe and contribute to a culture of safety, openness, and honesty. Without this, the group won't function successfully.
6. Accountability. Create an environment where the members own their recommendations and follow through on their promises.

Here are some specific responses:

Jean Lauterbach. "What strikes me as the most significant contribution of a chair is somewhere between a peer and a facilitator. It's the space where wisdom lies, wisdom that comes from not presuming to have the right answer so much as listening well enough (and with no preconceived agenda) to have the next question. Our members usually have the answers somewhere inside them, and patient, intentional listening will help them discover those answers and find the courage to make the hard decisions."

Janet Fogarty. "Chairs are somewhat like personal trainers. They help you get clarity on the goal, purpose, etc. and then keep you on course, push you and have your back. Chairs also hold the 'flashlight' and help a CEO or business owner identify, face, cope with, and influence the unknown. Chairs help leaders when their plans collide with reality."

Tony Lewis. "The Vistage chair is also an 'Equal' as well as a 'Peer' to the CEO member. For that reason, we take a trusting journey with the members to a 'Shared Destiny' in which the other members and we can say 'Time Out' anywhere along that journey. As Mark Twain said: 'It ain't what you don't know that gets you in trouble, but what you know that just ain't true.'"

Dwight Frindt. "A chair is a true friend, a partner, a committed listener, a provocateur, a pacesetter, someone to laugh with, sometimes be annoyed by, and sometimes a shoulder to cry on. A chair facilitates mutual trust, respect, and safety. A chair creates a broader paradigm for each person to discover and grow their unique leadership and develop clarity about their true calling. A chair is an everyday human being, who has discovered the true joy in service."

Phil Liebman. "As a chair, I am a catalyst. My job is to help lead and ideally accelerate a reaction (to opportunities, challenges, changes, or new observations about present realities) to produce better outcomes than would otherwise be the case—and do so without becoming part of the solution or final product. It is a way to leverage the power of people working unselfishly to a common purpose to make people's lives and the world a richer place. For me, it's about the power to help people understand that they can change what they want and certainly what they must, first in their company, then in their life and ultimately their communities and the world. I then renew and start the next reaction, then the next and the next. I see myself as both peer and expert, the same as I see every member in my groups."

Jean's comment reminds me of a quote from Khalil Gibran: "The teacher who is indeed wise does not bid you to enter the house of his wisdom but rather leads you to the threshold of your mind."[49]

Chapter Summary

The quotes from the Vistage chairs I had the privilege of joining for dinner espoused lessons, values, traits, and behaviors you'll find in any leadership book worth its salt. It's exactly what's involved when leading great teams in any organization. They prize clarity and transparency, lead by serving, are part of the team and not apart from it, care about relationships over transactions, and inspire rather than motivate; they are the types of leaders most people will follow to the ends of the earth.

In fairness to Roy, he was like a turtle: hard on the outside, soft on the inside. When he cared to show it, he had a big heart. Roy didn't lead people the way he did to be cruel; it was the only way he knew how. We don't have the luxury of that excuse. By thinking of our teams as triads where the leaders, the team, and individual members accept responsibility for the outputs and well as the outcomes, you'll have the start of a winning framework as you pursue Dave Logan's aspiration of living in the "Life Is Great" stage.

What's Next?

Now that the stage has been set, and the five factors have been reviewed in greater detail, it's time to look at the common challenges for each and share some thoughts on how to face them head-on. In doing so, we'll discover even more parallels between peer advisory groups and teams; we'll also get to the heart of what Peernovation is all about.

CHAPTER 7
Common Challenges and How to Meet Them

> Teamwork is the ability to work together toward a common vision. The ability to direct individual accomplishments toward organizational objectives. It is the fuel that allows common people to attain uncommon results.[50]
> —Andrew Carnegie

I LIKE TO THINK THAT THE POWER OF MY PEER ADVISORY GROUP workshop and its relevance to teams lies in the fact that I don't assess anything. I'm not there as a consultant. I simply guide people through conversations using the five factors as a framework; they reach conclusions based on their expectations and aspirations. There are two reasons for this. First, I approach this engagement as a student, as opposed to an expert in the field. Those who know me will tell you that I bristle when people refer to themselves experts. If someone else wants to call you that, feel free to let them, but the real experts I know remain students of their discipline first and never confer the expert moniker on themselves. It's how they develop their ever-evolving expertise and maintain their edge.

Second, being a group or team member is not a spectator sport. I'm not there so members can passively sit back and be taught. My role is to inspire them to reach their own conclusions and make commitments to one another that stand the test of time. If I approached it any other way, I'd be negating the very premise I am trying to espouse: the power of peers.

The Workshop Outline

I deliver a forty-five-minute presentation to set the stage, covering the pervasive nature of peer influence and how it has operated in our lives since birth. Through a combination of tapping into the audience's life experiences, sharing stories, and providing data, I make the case that peer influence is a force worth harnessing.

Peer advantage is being intentional about peer influence. It's to say, "What if you could take this powerful force and be more selective, strategic, and structured about the people you spend time with? What would that look like?" Together, we look at what peer advantage is capable of producing. The objective is to help them squeeze every ounce of value humanly possible out of their collective engagement. I do that by inviting them to explore the five factors, determine how they are performing in each area, and identify ways they can improve.

> **Peer advantage is being intentional about peer influence.**

In the next phase of the workshop, they look at each factor one at a time. Based on their expectations of one another and what they hope to achieve as individuals and for their organizations, they define their ideal state (10). Then, having established their ideal, they take stock of where they are today (on a scale of 1–10) and identify what it will take to bridge the gap for each factor. In other words, what will it take to get to 10?

In the final part of the workshop, they develop action items that will help them realize their ideal state and ultimately extract greater value from their experience. The five factors are as useful for cross-functional and departmental teams as they are for peer groups. Given the challenges we face ahead, particularly in a post-COVID-19 world, I believe sharing this work is vital for today's organizations.

Prevailing Results

Below, you'll find how peer groups ranked themselves on a scale of 1–10 for each of the five factors. Keep in mind that these are relative numbers and not necessarily appropriate for group-to-group comparison, which is why they appear in the aggregate. For example, a group that rated its productivity 8.5 isn't necessarily any more productive than another group that described themselves as a 7. The ratings are personal to each group based on their expectations and their tendencies to rank higher or lower on similar scales. While I did not identify individual groups, there's a great deal to be learned in general by looking at the mode for each factor (the number that appeared most often) and the challenges that were evident in most (if not all) groups.

HIGH LEVEL FINDINGS

How members have ranked themselves on each factor on a scale of 1-10 (*Mode):

- Factor 1 – **RIGHT PEERS** 7.5
- Factor 2 – **SAFETY** 9.5
 (Yet when asked how well members leverage that safe environment, the number drops to 6.5)
- Factor 3 – **PRODUCTIVITY** 7
- Factor 4 – **ACCOUNTABILITY** 6.5
- Factor 5 – **LEADERSHIP** 8

*Mode - The number that has been determined by a group most often for each factor

Figure 13. Aggregate ranking for each factor

Figure 14 offers the most common challenges by factor. We will explore them together one at a time and look at how some leaders and group members address them. The hope is that if your group experiences a similar challenge, you'll find some thought-starters to help you address it.

HIGH LEVEL FINDINGS

Common Challenges Associated With Each Factor

- **RIGHT PEERS** — Too few members, lack of diversity, attendance, preparation, engagement
- **PSYCHOLOGICAL SAFETY** — A member's unwillingness or inability to leverage a safe envirnment is a result of both listening and sharing models and a lack of camaraderie with the other members.
- **PRODUCTIVITY** — Members not bringing enough issues. The Issue Processing (IP) discipline is either too cumbersome or too rushed (lack of clarifying questions).
- **ACCOUNTABILITY** — Lacking both in therms of IP follow-up and with attendance, preparation, commitment, etc.
- **LEADERSHIP** — Members not being challenged enough

Figure 14. Common challenges for each factor

Challenges for Identifying and Recruiting the Right Peers

Committed members. If you believe larger groups work better, great. Just don't create a large group because you're thinking that if you have sixteen members and only ten show up, then at least you have enough people for the meeting to be productive. This approach presents a false narrative because inconsistent attendance will always keep your group from maximizing its potential.

While members may miss a meeting from time to time, the expectation should be that they prepare for the engagement, show up to the meeting, and are engaged while they are there. Anytime a member is absent, it compromises the group dynamic. Remember the story about Richard? Or can you imagine a great sports team where attending practice was optional? Having the right people is about having committed people, no matter how many members you believe to be ideal. Finding these members can be a challenge.

Who should be in the group? I've spoken to many groups with seven members who would like to add members so they can increase the diversity of perspectives that may be missing from their current conversations. Member diversity is defined in myriad ways (industry, practice area, race, age, gender, etc.). For example, the members might want to add more women or someone who represents manufacturing, professional services, or health care. In groups that operate in person, they typically want a membership that reflects their local community's demographics and local economy. Groups can struggle with identifying and recruiting participants who meet this goal.

Is diversity and inclusion enough? Values, and the behaviors that bring those values to life, rest at the core of a group's culture. Adding gender/racial diversity to the group, or new members who represent desired industry sectors, won't necessarily make the group stronger. They must also share the values existing members prize as being essential to bringing value to the group.

Group Action Items

During the workshop, I capture what the group has communicated regarding what it will take for them to achieve a 10 when it comes to having the right people. They reach an agreement on how many total members they want, the aspirational mix of the group, and the most important values they will share. I suggest they take time during one of their executive sessions to specify their ideal state further and develop a plan with timelines and shared responsibilities.

Revisiting this exercise provides more significant benefits than adding new members. Every time they talk about the shared values they expect from new members, the current members are implicitly making promises to each other about how they will show up to the group. This act alone has helped many groups raise their game more quickly than they thought possible.

Barriers to Psychological Safety

Accessing a Safe Environment. Just because the environment is safe doesn't mean everyone is maximizing its potential. Having the environment is one thing; inspiring members to take full advantage of it is quite another. We live in a world where we're regularly exposed to everyone's highlight reel, whether it's in person or on social media. When everything appears to be going great for everyone, we don't always find it easy to say we don't know something or to share that we're afraid of an impending challenge. Sharing what's really going on in our lives, as opposed to only what we want others to see, is an act of courage and generosity. Unlocking the group's ability to fully access the environment that's been created can be a daunting task and one that requires constant attention.

Business or personal? It's rare that I find members equally comfortable with talking about business and personal topics. One could argue that sharing business challenges as part of a business-focused mastermind group is a significant reason members join a group. For those groups where personal issues can dominate the conversation (at least for a time) because they impact a member's performance at work, new members are often surprised. I find it interesting that members will talk openly about their son's drug problem or their spouse's spending habits. Yet they are less willing to admit they made a mistake at work or concede they don't know something relative to their business. There is not a professional you and a personal you; there's just you. The more you bring your whole self to the group, the better for everyone.

Listening. Members who model good listening behaviors have a more significant impact on the willingness of others to share than those who model good sharing behaviors. While both are important, listening is a skill too often ignored. As a result, people are not always very good at it. Its impact on a safe environment has nothing to do with whether a member, if asked, could recall what someone just said. The question is, Does the degree to which people are listening match the gravity of the moment? No one wants to bare their soul to a roomful of people who are checking text messages or looking out the window. Being inattentive is how a safe environment gets compromised.

> **Does the degree to which people are listening match the gravity of the moment?**

Collegiality. Members suggest that while they see their fellow members for meetings every month (assuming excellent attendance, hence the reason it's important), they cite not knowing them well enough to open up (business or personal) as a reason for holding back. This situation suggests it takes more than getting together once a month to create a higher level of engagement.

Confidentiality. While, as stated earlier, I believe most groups do an exceptional job of honoring confidentiality, it cannot be taken for granted. On occasion, if a member isn't extra careful, it can be inadvertently compromised. Any time a new member joins a group, the comfort level about confidentiality drops a bit until the members get to know the new member better and earns the group's trust.

COMMON WAYS TO APPROACH CREATING PSYCHOLOGICAL SAFETY

Most of us simply don't have the conversational tools or the capacity to take full advantage of psychologically safe environments. Craig Weber's work on conversational capacity speaks to a group or team's ability to have open, balanced, non-defensive dialogue about difficult subjects.[51] Conversational capacity inspires trust. The more we trust, the more likely our conversational abilities will flourish.

Being open about both our business challenges as well as our personal ones can be liberating. The more willing we are to share what's going on in our lives, the better we can equip our peers to make a positive difference for us. That said, we're not all likely to do so at the same pace. This difference is where we have to be understanding of those who are predisposed to share and those who would self-identify as more private.

If you're a sharer, keep it up and model the way for others. If you're not, then take small steps. They may take you out of your comfort zone, but these steps will help you create a new one. Modeling good sharing behaviors is useful because it sets a positive example for others. Yet remember, it's the listeners who create the safety.

Building collegiality involves making an effort with a fellow group member beyond scheduled meetings that take place around a conference room table. Groups that create high levels of collegiality do so because they work at it. They meet for annual retreats, work together outside the meetings in triads or other small groups, and schedule social events (sometimes involving spouses) to forge deeper connections. Informal gatherings build emotional bridges that can help us unveil not just what we know but who we are and how we feel. Social gatherings are excellent practice fields for regularly scheduled group meetings.

Casual conversations outside the meeting about a confidential topic can happen. Just keep in mind that an innocent mention to a friend can quickly find its way into the public domain when your friend makes a casual remark to someone else. What happens in the room (or on Zoom) should stay there.

MAXIMIZING GROUP PRODUCTIVITY

Preparedness. Remember Helen? Helen's commitment to preparation helps her outshine every one of her members every month. (Hopefully by now, her fellow members are following suit). It's one of the traits of a productive group member that touches each of the five factors. You want to recruit people who take preparation seriously because if everyone shows up ready to play, everybody benefits. Who among us wants to be put in the hot seat if we're unprepared? That wouldn't feel very safe, would it? You can't share what you haven't prepared, and you can hardly expect your fellow members to prepare if you have not accepted personal responsibility to do so yourself. And group leaders who don't model good preparation behaviors shouldn't look for any followers.

Patience. Sometimes in life, slower is faster.[52] When I first heard about this concept, it made me think about receiving an item in the mail that required assembly. Rather than take the time to read a complex set of directions, I would dive right in. As a result, I often had to do it over several times. I either assembled the pieces in the wrong order, had parts left over that didn't seem to be too essential, or broke something because I tried to force it into place (sometimes all of the above). After countless failed attempts using this strategy over the years, I finally acquiesced to reading the directions and taking the process step-by-step.

The same holds for groups when they engage in a conversation about a complex problem, only to skip steps along the way. Skipping steps invariably makes the process drag on longer; worse yet, you help a member come up with the right answer to the wrong question. CEOs and key executives, being the problem-solvers they are, can tend to jump to the end prematurely.

Learning through follow-up. If a member commits to an action based on a conversation with the group but doesn't follow up with the group, then it's not only a lack of accountability; it's a lost learning opportunity. If I promised my group that I would take a specific action and, once I did, it resulted in something (positive or negative) that none of us anticipated during our prior conversation, it's up to me to share that. Remember, the power of we begins with me.

Imagination. Like any group or team, the process for engaging one another on challenging topics can be beneficial (issue processing), but it doesn't work for everything. Relying on it too frequently tends to compromise ways members can leverage the intellectual and emotional capital in the room. A systems-thinking approach would lead you to discover that using imagination to make the meeting more interesting also drives attendance. Why? Because the better the meetings, the less likely people will want to miss them. You could impose mandatory fines for members missing meetings, but you'd still be stuck with boring meetings. Instead, make the meeting a can't-miss experience. Consistently delivering on the latter may be more challenging, but it's a much more reliable and more sustainable approach.

> **Remember, the power of we begins with me.**

How Groups Can Be More Productive

Let's start with preparation. If there is one action item that offers the best opportunity for leverage in a group or team performance, it's preparation, which by itself is a game-changer. Reflect for a moment on the best and worst meetings you've ever attended. I'll bet the meetings that achieved the most significant outcomes involved well-prepared participants.

Preparation creates focus and sets the stage for more precise questions, better insights, and more potent takeaways, all in less time.

Preparation is also a two-way street. Let's say I plan to bring a complex issue to a group meeting. It not only means I should prepare my part, I also have to think about the background information I should make available to the other members. That way, they will have a baseline understanding of my topic before the meeting begins. Even if I'm prepared, if I don't do my job to get everyone else ready, I'll need to spend the first twenty minutes of our time together on information I could have provided in advance.

Preparing your fellow members gives them time to reflect on their own experiences and review content related to the subject area that will help them be of higher service. While any group agenda can always be subject to change, be sure to review the meeting agenda in advance and ask yourself what you need to be ready for the conversations that will likely take place. It allows you to bring the very best of you to the group.

Patience is synonymous with listening with the intent to frame precise questions, not to offer solutions before you understand the complete story. Groups help CEOs ask informed questions. It's no different from what we frequently experience in our personal lives. A friend calls and shares a predicament he may be having. After hearing the initial description of what's going on, I would never start blurting out solutions. I would ask clarifying questions about the situation, inquire as to what he's done about it to date, and, most importantly, not make the assumption that I know his desired outcome and why. Even then, while I might share relevant experiences, I would hope that the result of the conversation wasn't about me offering a solution, so much as guiding him to a decision he's comfortable with, one he takes ownership of. The more time you spend asking questions, the more likely and more quickly the right options will emerge.

Preparation instigates follow-up, and follow-up encourages learning. When you review notes from the last meeting to prepare for the next one, it gives you time to reflect on the conversations you had the previous month. Assuming you care about the outcomes of those conversations, you'll be poised to ask other relevant queries.

I've found that many group leaders have a wonderful imagination when it comes to leading meetings and trying different tools that can be effective in facilitating great conversations. As stated earlier, though, group membership is not a spectator sport. Members should feel free to access the talents within their group in myriad ways. Here are some popular suggestions for doing so:

Asking "What if …?" questions. What if an unlikely competitor disrupted my company's business? What if another pandemic strikes? Raising these questions and preparing for these scenarios will not only serve you; it will matter to every other member. In the wake of the 2008 financial crisis, mastermind group members across the world credited their groups for helping them survive and later thrive, as many of their competitors went out of business. As one member told me, "It wasn't that my company was better managed; it's that my group helped me be better prepared."

Questioning answers. Sometimes, it's helpful to think of your fellow members not in terms of getting your questions answered, so much as getting your answers questioned. If you had a tough decision to make that may not have involved the group, but you believe the story of how you reached the decision could be instructive, take time to share it. Better yet, if you haven't implemented it yet, it's a great time to ask, "What am I missing?"

Presentation. If you have a major presentation, whether it's to your employees, board of directors, or an important client, then consider asking your members to serve as a mock audience. Giving the presentation a trial run with your group will help you and everyone else. Whenever I've seen this done, the presenter gets fantastic coaching, and everyone else in the room takes notes about the things they should and shouldn't do the next time they come across a similar situation. It's a huge win-win.

Role-Playing. Imagine a hard conversation you may need to have with a client or employee. Preparing a fellow member and role-playing that communication for the group can be an effective way to practice the words and temper the emotions that may likely be involved. Again, you get practice, you get coached, and everyone else benefits as well.

ACCOUNTABILITY

The relationship between safety and accountability. It's one thing to experience a real aha moment regarding the correlation between psychological safety and the ability to hold ourselves accountable, but it's not enough. The challenge is how to use accountability to elevate safety and leverage safety to enhance member-to-member accountability, making it part of the fabric of the group.

Accountability for shared values. When you ask group members to define what accountability means for a mastermind group, their heads always go to following up with members on promises made to the group. While that's part of it, they don't tend to hold themselves or one another accountable for shared values and behaviors nearly often enough. These values might include attendance, preparation, engagement, learning versus judging, confidentiality, accepting personal responsibility, being transparent, being willing to challenge others, and staying open to being challenged. It's among the many reasons that a lack of accountability and failure to leverage existing psychological safety can keep a group from growing.

Proper mechanisms. Too many groups lack the mechanisms to realize member-to-member accountability consistently, and they are not always aware of the practices and tools available to them.

How to Make Member-to Member Accountability Possible

Creating a culture of member-to-member accountability is a challenge for a whole host of reasons. First, it's not as if the leader of the group can impose a culture of accountability among members. Second, how do the members define accountability for themselves? What should it look like? Third, where does member-to-member accountability start, if not with the leader?

If you recall the leadership triad from chapter 6, it's based on the idea that the leader, the group, and the individual member are all responsible for whatever attribute you want to put in the middle, including accountability. Just because the leader is at the top of the triad doesn't necessarily mean that's where it starts. It's almost paradoxical to imagine the leader serving as the enforcer of member-to-member accountability. To understand how leaders play the part of the backstop rather than the enforcer, see figure 15.

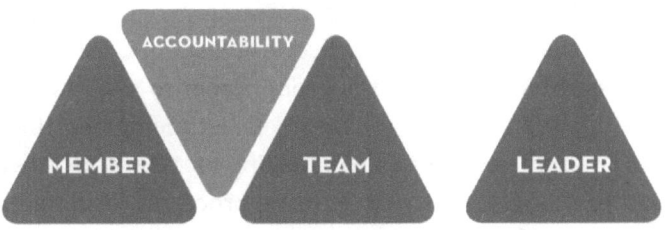

Figure 15. Group accountability model

The proper sequencing of how member-to-member accountability occurs requires taking the top off the triangle and placing it on the far right, with accountability resting where it belongs, between the individual member and the group. This dynamic is valid for two reasons: 1) Members who believe the power of we begins with me accept it as their responsibility to serve as a model of accountability to others. 2) Once members assume that role, they initiate the accountability conversations with group support.

Think of it this way: If I sought help from the group on a particular challenge, and after our conversation, I committed to taking specific action steps, it would be up to me to share the status. If nothing else, I would do so out of gratitude to the group. If I somehow got distracted by something on my way to the meeting and failed to update everyone, another member (who presumably came prepared) would likely follow up. On the off chance I didn't raise the issue, and not one person asked, then the leader of the group would play the role of the backstop. She would gently (or not so gently) remind the group that it should never have gotten that far. Member-to-member accountability rests between the individual and the group. Addressing the common challenges is up to them, along with the depth and breadth of accountability they wish to create.

How Groups Challenge Leadership

Challenge the members. By far, the most frequently voiced feedback from members to the leaders of their groups is to challenge them more. This feedback does not suggest that the leader isn't challenging the members already, but as stated earlier, high-performing people are hungry for a challenge, and they want to be coached.

Follow-up. Members want the group leader to assist with peer-to-peer follow-up, and for the chair to set aside time during the meeting to do so. It's mainly playing a role in helping members help themselves, as opposed to doing it for them. Finding processes, technologies, and strategies that work for the group as a whole, especially when new members join the group, can also be a challenge.

Preparation help. Members understand that they need to prepare, yet they can't do it entirely alone. While they can undoubtedly review material and consult with their fellow members to develop and create continuity from one meeting to the next, the chair drives the meeting agenda. Members want help preparing for what's next.

Speaker topics. Many mastermind groups bring guest speakers to their meetings to deliver timely and valuable content aimed at helping members grow their businesses. Members want a voice in identifying relevant topics that can help the chair select the best thought leaders and speakers available in each suggested subject area.

Chapter Summary

Examining the mastermind group workshop, Harnessing Peer Advantage to Your Advantage, and crawling inside each of the five factors is an essential exercise for groups and teams alike. By understanding the common challenges more clearly, it's easy to see the parallels between group and teams, and realize how groups serve as useful practice fields for CEOs and key executives alike.

What's Next?

Now that we've reviewed the challenges and covered some of the ways groups meet these challenges, it's time to show you how all this connects to building high-performing teams in your organization and start you on your journey from me to we.

CHAPTER 8
What Peernovation Means for Teams and the Journey from Me to We

> The nice thing about teamwork is that you
> always have others on your side.
> —Margaret Carty[53]

IN THE LATE 1990S, I RAN MY FIRST MARATHON. I WANTED TO RUN one and only one. Of course, for whatever reason, I completed another twelve marathons over the next few years and had a fantastic time doing it. More than the marathon itself, I enjoyed the discipline of the training programs, which usually covered eighteen weeks from day one to race day.

I followed Hal Higdon's marathon training programs. One of the big running thrills of my life was joining him in northeast Florida for a three-miler along the beach. Today, Hal is eighty-eight years old, having written thirty-four books and completed more than 110 marathons. This wonderful man comes to mind because to start his training program, you had to be at a certain fitness level, which included being able to run a least seven miles before you began training. I think the same is true for Peernovation. You can't just jump off the sofa and dive in; you have to do some evaluation and prework before you decide to bring Peernovation into your organization. Let me explain.

Getting Started

The difference between my work with mastermind groups and organizational teams is worth noting if you plan to take Peernovation and try this at home, if you will. First, the cultures one finds in today's companies vary far more significantly than what I tend to see when I visit CEO groups. Using Dave Logan's five stages of culture, described in chapter 6, I would regard most of the groups as living in Stage 4, no matter which organization is running them or who is leading them. This means, according to Logan's research, that roughly three-quarters of companies today would find embracing Peernovation rather challenging.

> You can't just jump off the sofa and dive in

A company at Stage 5, "Life Is Great," practices its own brand of Peernovation and likely pushes its boundaries. Organizations living in Stages 1–3, however, are more apt to display variations of command-and-control leadership. In most cases, these cultures would struggle with Peernovation because they would fall short on each of the five factors necessary for making such collaboration possible. That said, if you want to move to Stage 4 because you want to create the kind of safe environment that will give your employees a voice, then here's how to get started. Let me share a construct for your people and you as the CEO that will help you assess your cultural fitness and prepare you for bringing Peernovation to your place of business.

A Construct for Listening and Sharing

About ten years ago, I developed a short presentation for a Seton Hall University symposium in Phoenix, covering an important topic for the senior-level executives in attendance. The title was "Speaking Truth to Power." The presentation included a brief history of the subject, which, as you can imagine, included everything from "kill the messenger," an idea expressed by Sophocles in 442 BC, to the work of the late Warren Bennis, who counseled Democratic and Republican presidents alike, from Kennedy to Reagan.

While there are countless books about leadership, followership by comparison gets short shrift. In speaking of followership, Bennis wrote, "In a world of growing complexity, leaders are increasingly dependent on their subordinates for good information, whether the leaders want to hear it or not. Followers who tell the truth, and leaders who listen to it are an unbeatable combination."[54]

For Peernovation to grow and flourish, it's essential to plant it in a culture where this unbeatable combination Bennis wrote about is at least an aspirational goal of the CEO. The first half of the twenty-point construct you're about to review was developed in 2010. The second half was crafted just over a year ago to address the phenomenon that it's the listeners who create the safety, and it's up to the CEO to model the listening behaviors she expects of others. Why? Because, as we know, the CEO is part of the team, not apart from it. Speaking truth to power takes courage and humility for all involved. Let's examine what it takes for the employee and then for the CEO to engage in a fruitful dialogue on a difficult subject.

> **While there are countless books about leadership, followership by comparison gets short shrift.**

Here's the short version of my advice to employees delivered at the symposium:

1. **Trust yourself.** Have confidence in your expertise, your understanding of the situation, and the recommendations you're providing.
2. **Consider it your responsibility to share your professional judgment.** It's what you're paid to do.
3. **Know your audience.** Organize and frame the information in a fashion that's compelling and has the best chance of being heard.
4. **Be prepared.** Anticipate all questions. If you're going to present an idea or action, be ready to defend it.
5. **Make your point succinctly,** and don't bury the lead. Offer the headline and provide the supporting evidence, not the other way around.

6. **Do so in the broader interest, not self-interest.** Consider speaking truth to power as an organizational imperative, never a personal one.
7. **Persuade.** Deliver your message with passion, and be sure you are clearly understood. Don't take a ceremonial position.
8. **Be patient.** You may not get an immediate response, so allow your CEO to chew on what you said for a while.
9. **Understand that bad news is better coming from you than from the outside.**
10. **Trust your leadership.** If the CEO doesn't take your recommendation, know that she recognizes your lens on the situation, and you should trust hers.

In 2019, I built on the first ten points and developed a guide to help CEOs create the kind of psychological safety necessary for an employee to speak truth to power successfully.

1. **Trust your people.** Trust that when they come to you, they are giving you their best judgment based on their expertise and vantage point.
2. **You hired them for a reason.** Staying quiet is not what you hired them to do. You need their best thinking to be vocalized in real-time. This is something to applaud, not discourage.
3. **Know your employee.** Be mindful of why your employee is coming to you.
4. **Be patient.** Speaking truth to the CEO (or any leader) can be stressful enough without making them feel that they have ten seconds to capture your attention.
5. **Be open to listening.** Take time to fully understand the point of view they are sharing and why they feel so strongly about it.
6. **After you've listened, use appreciative inquiry to learn more.** By all means, pressure-test their position, but do so in a supportive fashion, without putting them on the defensive.
7. **Consider it your default position that their motives are in the broader interest and not personal.** It's critical to give them

the benefit of the doubt here. If they are operating in their self-interest, it won't take a brain surgeon to figure it out.
8. **Don't feel the need to respond in the moment.** Thank your employee for coming to you. If you need to give it more thought and gather more information, by all means, do so. That said, follow up with the employee directly as soon as practical.
9. **If it's bad news, thank your employee for sharing it with you.** Better you hear it from the inside first, before it comes at you from the outside.
10. **Since you advised your employee to trust you, keep their unique vantage point in mind.** They are giving you the best recommendation they can based on the information they have. This is a gift. Show your employee how much you appreciate it.

If you believe you can create the kind of environment for yourself as the CEO and for the other leaders in your organization that inspires this kind of dialogue (or you already have), then you're ready to start the program.

A Word About Consequences

A second difference between mastermind groups and company teams is that there are consequences for team members who test the boundaries of psychological safety; such consequences don't exist for group members. Group members aren't paid or able to get promoted or demoted from the group (at least not too often). If you're trying to create a culture of transparency and sharing, then employees can't believe that if they ask the hard questions or share an unpopular idea, that it will cost them money or status in the organization.

I've shared this story many times, but it's hard to imagine a more powerful illustration of what it took to create a culture of psychological safety in the face of perceived consequences than Alan Mulally's tenure at Ford Motor Co. As Ford's CEO, Mulally would lead meetings that involved his senior leadership team, where they reported on their dashboards. They would say green if they were on track, yellow to signal caution, and red if there was trouble. Ford was losing $17 billion at the time, and as Mulally called on the leaders to share their dashboards, they all reported showing green across the board. Imagine being the CEO, who just took charge of a company that was losing $17 billion and receiving feedback from your senior team that everything is firing on all cylinders. Could there be worse news?

Before Mulally took over, the culture at Ford was one that did not tolerate public admissions to problems. Admitting that you couldn't handle something on your own was a ticket out the door. As much as Mulally encouraged his team to speak up, they couldn't bring themselves to do it. One day, one of the team members raised his hand and said, "Hey, I've got a problem over here, and I could use some advice."

Mulally stood up and applauded, and the team proceeded to address this leader's concern. It took time, patience, and hard work on both sides to develop an environment of psychological safety, but over time people collaborated as never before. By the way, the company's performance improved rather famously, and the first person who was brave enough to admit he had a problem that needed to be addressed by the team succeeded Mulally as the CEO.

Individual Benefits versus a Collective Work Product

The third significant difference between working with mastermind groups and teams involves how they are different, and what Peernovation means in the context of each. To review, *groups* convene to help individual members achieve their goals. *Teams* work together toward achieving a collective goal or creating a shared work product. *Peernovation* occurs when a carefully selected group of people, who share a common purpose and values, work together to make each other better and create something larger than themselves.

For groups, the "larger than themselves" aspect of giving to others and making a difference in someone else's life is different from creating a common work product for which everyone shares very directly in the outcome. The former speaks to what we regard as being better to give than to receive, yet realizing that giving to others reaps its satisfaction and rewards. The latter involves Harry S. Truman's famous quote, "It's amazing what you can accomplish if you don't care who gets the credit."[55] For teams, this is where trust begins rather than ends. It's human nature to want to amplify the role you as an individual may have played in any team victory. Organizational recognition and monetary rewards only exacerbate the problem. Creating a culture where credit is always shared involves individual discipline and company systems at every level that reinforce a culture of Peernovation.

Applying Group Findings to Teams

Despite some significant differences, I'm sure you've already connected the dots regarding the relevance of the findings from peer advisory groups and how they may apply to your organization. Let's review the challenges one by one.

The Right People

When you look at the common challenges for recruiting the right peers for a high-performing group, it's eerily similar to the daunting task of hiring the right person to fill a position on a team at your organization. Finding people who are passionate and committed to being at their very best in pursuit of achieving organizational goals can be difficult, no matter how many interviews or assessments you conduct. Still, how many organizations out there develop hiring criteria that is so specific, it eliminates someone who may not fit the mold you created yet could bring extraordinary talents and skills to the team?

> *For companies, hiring is typically a two-step process, a process of elimination and a process of selection.*

Groups find recruiting difficult because of scarcity; companies find it challenging because of abundance. For companies, hiring is typically a two-step process, a process of elimination and a process of selection. During the elimination process, the goal is to discard as many of the four hundred resumes that may be on file for a specific position as humanly possible. Often, there's nothing human about it at all; just keyword searches. By the time you enter the selection process, after eliminating countless candidates who could have been great additions to your team, you have no better pool of candidates to choose from than the leader of a mastermind group. Hence the problem with achieving both professional diversity and cultural fit.

Psychological Safety

While groups have the challenge of creating a safe environment and having to show members how to access it, company teams often lack psychological safety from the start. To be fair, creating psychological safety for teams is more laborious and, in some workplace cultures, next to impossible. It mainly has to do with hierarchy and the perceived consequences that come with speaking up, speaking out, or taking risks. (It's why I mentioned the concept of prework.) When you consider the exhaustive and expensive process of hiring the right people, it's mind-boggling, right? Hire the perfect employees, only to put them in a box and never allow them to deliver their truly unique insights and gifts to the organization, just cogs in the wheel. When these same employees and CEOs join a mastermind group, they either find sharing so challenging or discover the experience so liberating that they are a group's most open participants.

Productivity in Teams

You have these talented people who now enjoy an environment where everyone is feeling a higher level of psychological safety. How do you know they are as productive as they can be? The increase in people working from home in 2020 due to COVID-19 has shined a new light on collaboration and productivity. What would happen if you eliminated a two-hour daily commute and added more time to everyone's day? What would happen if people worked from home more often and, by definition, invited their fellow employees virtually into their homes? Would a window into our shared humanity drive more cooperative collaboration and increase productivity? We have been forced into this reality, but we can learn from it as well. Be prepared, learn from one another through collaboration and follow-up, and be patient with each other. Slower is faster with teams as well.

Accountability in Teams

Team members are typically doing one of two things: playing offense or playing defense. On the accountability front, you want them to play offense as much as possible. Great employees and world-class athletes typically hold themselves to a higher standard than their managers or coaches. These are the people you want on your team. They'll do what it takes, and best of all, they love to be challenged and coached. Create a shared commitment to values and behaviors, and let the power of peers take over. Their currency and their responsibility rest with each other. The challenge is switching from employees who are accustomed to playing defense, as they are relentlessly being held accountable by their bosses, to accepting responsibility for setting new standards of excellence for their work.

Leading Teams

Renowned education expert Linda Darling-Hammond from Stanford mentioned during a podcast appearance in 2017 that when teachers collaborate, they are more effective at creating collaborative environments among their students in the classroom. This fact is true for CEOs and business leaders as well. It's one of the passive learning experiences that are among the most valuable benefits of being part of a peer advisory group. It's your practice field for learning how to lead more collaborative teams at your organization. It's also something to bring inside your company, as peer groups (practice fields) inside your organization will not only drive greater collaboration and alignment, but also serve as a mechanism for operationalizing your investment in learning and development.

Looking Ahead

People have been learning and growing together in mastermind groups for quite some time now. Whether you look to Benjamin Franklin's Junto, Napoleon Hill's depiction of the Vagabonds (a mastermind group that included Henry Ford, Thomas Edison, President Warren G. Harding, and Harvey Firestone), or the first TEC group started in 1957 by Bob Nourse, these groups have proved to be remarkably effective. I believe the evolution of mastermind groups will be a harbinger for how organizational teams grow in the future. Let's look at what's the same, what's different, and how you can make Peernovation possible for your team.

What Will Stay the Same

No matter how your group meets or how often, the five factors common to high-performing peer advisory groups will be a constant:

Right peers. Having the right peers involves how they are similar and different. Groups need a common domain shared by all members.[56] This domain may involve each member being a CEO or COO, a woman business owner, and so on, a common platform or purpose, if you will. While they also need to share common values, their differences are essential to the group's power of perspective. Members bring their successes, failures, biases, and range of experiences. It's this mix of similarities and differences that gives a group its unique identity and purpose.

Safe environment. There's a great deal of evidence to support the need for psychological safety for peer groups and teams. For groups, this manifests in terms of believing the environment is safe to share ideas without fear of being judged, where one can divulge sensitive information.

Group members cannot function properly in an environment they believe to be unsafe. Psychological safety is to the group what oxygen is to human survival.

Productivity. Groups need to engage in valuable interaction that gleans tangible outcomes. If they do so effectively, they will grow. Members will be challenged to continually pressure-test their safe environment by bringing weighty topics to the group and participating in deep conversations that lead to positive outcomes.

Accountability. Top peer groups and teams (sports or business) have a culture of accountability among their members. They share expectations of what showing up as a good member looks like. These expectations include being committed to the group's success and bringing their best to every engagement. It's what drives the group to be better, and it's what creates the criteria for any new member who wishes to enjoy the privilege of being part of it.

Leadership. Leadership can mean everything from having a trained facilitator lead the group, to a member who serves as the leader, to members who rotate leadership of the group. That said, the role is ostensibly the same: lead to support the group's success and accept the position as steward of the factors outlined above.

What Will Change

While the five factors will remain the same, much will change. (It's already happening.) Here are just a few thoughts:

More hybrid formats. In my work as an adjunct professor over the past decade, I've found it's tough to beat the educational experience one realizes through participation in a course that involves both in-person and online student engagements. The same holds for peer groups and teams. Combine the spontaneity of the synchronous setting (in-person or virtual) with the thoughtful dialogue that occurs in an asynchronous online experience, and watch the magic happen. Both provide

> **Advances in online conversational video platforms such as Circles will make virtual meetings even more practical.**

opportunities for students or business leaders to learn from one another and develop deep bonds. The groups and teams of the future will blend these types of engagements in exciting new ways. This development will not only open doors and extend their reach, but also eliminate geographic and time constraints that have kept too many leaders from adopting these practices to date.

Frequency and length of meetings. Fixed monthly all-day and half-day meetings are being joined by models where members meet more frequently for less time. (Many traditional peer advisory groups have already adapted these models, at least temporarily, to help their members help one another through the pandemic). While there's something to be said for all-day and half-days away from the office to work *on* your business rather than *in* it, there's also value in the accessibility that's afforded by today's emerging peer advisory group models. If you can make it an *and* not an *either or*, you'll find value in joining both. Utilizing the hybrid model above, we'll see more in-person meetings taking place less frequently (a handful of times a year). Online video conferencing will occur more often, likely twice a month, for ninety minutes to two hours max. Advances in online conversational video platforms such as Circles will make virtual meetings even more practical.

Content (applied). Bringing speakers in for half-day and full-day workshops will take a back seat to more efficient and practical content delivery. For example, picture sixty-minute specially designed webinars led by the likes of Daniel Goleman, Cynthia Montgomery, and Simon Sinek. The thing is, they won't just parrot their books; they'll show group members how to apply their concepts in the real world. Sharing such content among hundreds or even thousands of groups makes this far less expensive and infinitely more scalable. Moreover, groups will develop mechanisms for reinforcing what they've learned over time, thus giving members the capacity and courage to apply it with greater success.

More asynchronous engagement and learning. Being at your best starts with showing up prepared for every meeting. The availability of well-curated written, audio, and video material between sessions, supported by asynchronous online conversation boards, will inspire more continual learning and sharing. These platforms offer a powerful forum for fruitful dialogue and reflection.

The Journey from Me to We

The case for bringing Peernovation to your organization, assuming your leadership and your culture are ready, willing, and able, is based on ten immutable truths:

1. We exist in systems, not siloes.
2. We each possess ladders of inference and mental models that limit our perspective.
3. The more we are open to climbing another person's ladder, the broader our perspective.
4. The broader our perspective, the more we see and understand.
5. None of us is as smart as all of us.
6. We learn better when we learn together.
7. The learning-achieving cycle is the key to growth and innovation.
8. Achieving a robust learning-achieving cycle involves five factors.
9. The five factors are not pillars; they are a reinforcing loop.
10. A great team can accomplish the extraordinary.

I hope that you desire to accomplish the extraordinary. Doing so will require a commitment to hiring the right people, people who share a passion for your business, embrace the values you hold dear, and provide a diversity of experiences that will broaden your organizational perspective. It will involve a Herculean effort to creating psychological safety at every level, building an environment that maximizes productivity, and encouraging a culture of accountability among team members. From a leadership perspective, it will require a selfless commitment to serving your teams the same way mastermind group members help one another.

Doing so will benefit everyone involved: employees, clients, customers, shareholders, vendors, your families, and the countless other people responsible for making your organization even possible. To get you started, visit Peernovation.co/teams, where you'll find a free PDF with detailed notes that you can use to deliver a Peernovation primer to your team. Feel free to run with it on your own. If you want help, I know a guy.

Enjoy!

No one can whistle a symphony. It takes a whole orchestra to play it.[57]
—H. E. Luccock

AFTERWORD

Peernovation focuses on what makes us uniquely human, and how we work and learn better when we do it together. As we look to the future of work, Leo Bottary asked me to write about something you'll be adding to your team soon if you haven't already: Artificial Intelligence (AI).

As I reflected on the many stories Leo tells throughout the book, one of the anecdotes that struck me was from his workshop, when he asked CEOs to identify the very best team they have ever been part of and what made it so great. It was amazing how many of those CEOs picked teams from back in high school or even earlier.

When I think about this in the context of utilizing artificial intelligence, I realize that with AI, I too can begin to recall past high school experiences with much greater clarity but now from the individual perspective of all the people who were present in my memories.

Artificial intelligence can generate evidence-based assumptions of each person in your high school memory, based on all the publicly and privately available information about that person. AI is capable of understanding and cognitively connecting many different events, facts, lost details, and seemingly unrelated elements of a person's past. It can put together a personality profile of each person in your memory, with a certain level of accuracy, depending upon your requirements, and then it can replay that same memory but now from the unique perspectives of each of the individuals in your memory!

How incredibly important and helpful would all your memories of your interactions with your peers be?

With artificial intelligence, you would be naturally learning from your memory plus the memories of your peers in your memory. What were they experiencing at that moment? What were they thinking about? This is not clairvoyant mind-reading; these are data-based assumptions that AI has made based on your peers' available actions, statements, and life choices from that moment in high school until now.

Artificial intelligence will play an incredible role in your life. Its primary role and function is to help you. It will supplement you with additional advice, recommendations, and facts, but it will not ever replace you.

Artificial intelligence will give you so much more information from so many more resources that are inaccessible to you today. AI will access data that is written in a foreign language and data that is archived in some hidden subfile in a long-forgotten remote server.

Over time, you and your peers will become dependent on artificial intelligence. You will want to access it all the time, with its almost-limitless ability to access and process information with the sole objective to help you make the right decision.

Even with this dependency, artificial intelligence will not replace you. AI is just lines of computer code running on a computer. You are not. You are a human being: flawed, confused, irrational, insecure, paranoid, jealous, and so on. Your unique flaws are your uncodeable strengths. Your flaws are the reason why you fall in love with a person who makes absolutely no sense to anyone but you.

We are all intimately interlocked with one another: the feelings you share when you see someone you love, the emotions you feel when your eyes lock, and at that moment, your souls become further intertwined and inseparable. That spontaneous experience is what makes you human, and those powerful experiences are the catalyst that drives the human race.

Even though people created artificial intelligence, we cannot program our quintessential basic human traits. The role of AI and its incredible benefits, its superiority in remembering things, accessing things, and continuously helping you, is critical to our advancement, but it cannot and will not replace you being human.

Our future, as a team of peers, will definitively include artificial intelligence. You will not have to type or speak out loud to communicate with it. You'll just have to think it, and the AI will have already processed your request and thoughts.

Our future teams of peers will be humans and AI, but you won't call it AI. It will just be there, integrated seamlessly, invisible but still present.

As it was before and will be in the future, the only people in the room will be you and your peers because we are irreplaceable. So, don't resist the Peernovation that is already here.

Thomas F. Anglero
Nordic Director of Innovation at IBM

ACKNOWLEDGMENTS

The two years since writing *What Anyone Can Do* has been a time for discovery, both personally and professionally. Personally, I've become increasingly accustomed to the wonders of being a grandparent. Nora is three, and Ben is just over a year old. Whatever we can do to make the world a better place for them and their peers will be a function of our ability to work together more effectively than we ever have.

I discovered the joy of a new relationship. My wife, Diane, is the most beautiful and loving person I've ever known. Diane sees the best in everyone, as does her son Darren, daughter Noelle, sisters Linda and Sue, and her amazing parents, Jack and Jean; we celebrated their seventieth wedding anniversary together in the spring of 2019. How's that for the power of peers? My daughters Kristin and Taylor, my dad (James) and his wife Cheryl, my brother Jim, his wife Karen, and their adult children Amanda, Jimmy, and John, all celebrated our October 2019 wedding at Esperanza in Cabo San Lucas. To watch two families so seamlessly become one could be the subject of another book. Now we're just one big dream team. I appreciate their love, encouragement, support, critiques, and editing skills.

Professionally speaking, I've tested the latest iteration of the five factors for high-performing groups and teams throughout North America and the United Kingdom, learning from each experience and fine-tuning my workshop every step of the way. It's been a four-year process that's given birth to Peernovation (both the company and the concept). In the new workplace, artificial intelligence (AI) will coexist with people (as

Thomas Anglero explained in the Afterword), meaning that our ability to bring our collective humanity to an everchanging equation will be essential to meeting its unique challenges. With this book, I hope to kick-start a collaborative movement that spreads across the world.

I appreciate the assistance of the teams at Vistage Worldwide (San Diego), Vistage UK, Vistage Florida, TEC Canada, and their chairs and members, all of whom lead, participate, and support amazing peer advisory groups for CEOs, small business owners, and key executives. These groups provided the laboratory for many of the findings that have been advanced since writing *The Power of Peers* (2016) and *What Anyone Can Do* (2018).

My longtime friend Marty Lynch, a new friend Alexander Keehnen, Kristine Ochu (W.I.N. Mastermind group member), and my partner in crime Randy Cantrell, who introduced me to the world of podcasting and has been a wonderful content collaborator since 2016, all made invaluable contributions to this narrative. Emily Christensen (Paper Cake Creative) prepared the cover art, illustrations, and photographs for publication. I also want to thank my Learning Team (LT21) from the Master of Arts in Strategic Communication & Leadership program and our professors at Seton Hall University. After more than a decade, I continue to draw from my experiences with them every day.

I want to acknowledge the support of Jeffrey Hayzlett, author and part-time cowboy, who is as generous a person I know and who graciously agreed to write the foreword. Thanks to Jennifer Vessels, founder of Executive Growth Alliance, who taught me a great deal and introduced me to Thomas F. Anglero, Nordic Director of Innovation at IBM. Thomas's grasp of the power of technology is exceeded only his understanding of and optimism about people. I thank Thomas for writing the afterword and providing us with a fitting launching pad for what's next.

ABOUT THE AUTHOR

 Leo Bottary is the founder and managing partner of Peernovation, LLC. He is a sought-after thought leader on peer advantage and Peernovation, emerging disciplines dedicated to strategically engaging peers to achieve personal and organizational excellence. A popular author, keynote speaker, and workshop facilitator, he also serves as an instructor for Rutgers University and opinion columnist for *CEOWORLD Magazine*. Leo's first book, which he coauthored with former Vistage CEO Leon Shapiro, *The Power of Peers: How the Company You Keep Drives Leadership Growth & Success* (2016), explored how and why formal peer groups for CEOs and business leaders are so effective. His second book, *What Anyone Can Do: How Surrounding Yourself with the Right People Will Drive Change, Opportunity, and Personal Growth* (2018), examined the power of enlisting and engaging the complete circle of the people who surround us in both formal and informal settings.

Prior to teaching at Rutgers, Leo was an adjunct professor at Seton Hall University, where he led graduate-level online and on-campus learning teams studying leadership and strategic communication. In April 2015, he was named adjunct teacher of the year for Seton Hall's College of Communication and the Arts.

Earlier in his career, Leo served in senior leadership positions at Mullen and Hill & Knowlton, where he was also director of client service for the US. In the mid-1990s, he founded a public relations agency that a leading trade publication hailed as a regional powerhouse, new media pioneer, and great place to work. Leo earned a BA from Jacksonville University and an MA in Strategic Communication and Leadership from Seton Hall University, and he completed his doctoral coursework at Northeastern University.

NOTES

1. "A Quote by Kenneth H. Blanchard." Goodreads. Accessed June 2, 2020. https://www.goodreads.com/quotes/56863-none-of-us-is-as-smart-as-all-of-us.
2. "A Quote by Kenneth H. Blanchard." Goodreads. Accessed June 2, 2020. https://www.goodreads.com/quotes/56863-none-of-us-is-as-smart-as-all-of-us.
3. Peter M. Senge, *The Fifth Discipline: The Art and Practice of the Learning Organization* (New York: Doubleday/Currency, 1990), 3.
4. "Digital Media Literacy: What Is an Echo Chamber?" GCFGlobal.org. Accessed April 26, 2020. https://edu.gcfglobal.org/en/digital-media-literacy/what-is-an-echo-chamber/1/.
5. Leo Bottary, "An Open Letter to Cable News." Vistage Research Center. Vistage Worldwide, May 5, 2011. https://www.vistage.com/research-center/business-leadership/strategic-communications/an-open-letter-to-cable-n/.
6. Leon Shapiro and Leo Bottary, *The Power of Peers: How the Company You Keep Drives Leadership, Growth & Success* (Boston: Bibliomotion, 2016).
7. Bersin, Josh. "The Power of Collaborative Learning: More Important Than Ever." May 20, 2019. https://joshbersin.com/2019/05/the-power-of-collaborative-learning-more-important-than-ever/.
8. Michael Goodman, "Systems Thinking: What, Why, When, Where, and How?" *The Systems Thinker*, August 16, 2016. https://thesystemsthinker.com/systems-thinking-what-why-when-where-and-how/.
9. "A Quote by Helen Keller." Goodreads. Accessed June 2, 2020. https://www.goodreads.com/quotes/9411-alone-we-can-do-so-little-together-we-can-do.
10. "*Apollo 13* Quotes." Movie Quotes.com. Accessed April 26, 2020. https://www.moviequotes.com/s-movie/apollo-13/.
11. Apollo 13 Mission Report (Houston, September 1970).

12. Stanford University. "Text of Steve Jobs' Commencement Address (2005)." *Stanford News*, June 12, 2017. https://news.stanford.edu/2005/06/14/jobs-061505/.
13. Gene Kranz, personal communication, April 1996.
14. Leo Bottary, *What Anyone Can Do: How Surrounding Yourself with the Right People Will Drive Change, Opportunity, and Personal Growth* (New York: Routledge, 2019).
15. *How Wolves Change Rivers*. Sustainable Human. February 13, 2014. Accessed May 08, 2020. https://www.youtube.com/watch?v=ysa5OBhXz-Q.
16. Editor, *Business News Daily*. "Business Advice from Albert Einstein: Business Tips." businessnewsdaily.com, April 19, 2012. https://www.businessnewsdaily.com/2381-albert-einstein-business-tips.html.
17. Peter Checkland, "Systems Theory and Management Thinking," *Critical Issues in Systems Theory and Practice* (1995), 1–14. https://doi.org/10.1007/978-1-4757-9883-8_1.
18. "Briefing Paper One: Systems Thinking." Systems Thinking. Accessed April 26, 2020. http://www.reallylearning.com/Free_Resources/Systems_Thinking/systems_thinking.html.
19. William Braun, "The System Archetypes" (February 27, 2002).
20. Peter M. Senge, *The Fifth Discipline: The Art & Practice of the Learning Organization* (Rev. ed.) (New York: Doubleday, 2006).
21. Braun, "The System Archetypes."
22. Senge, *The Fifth Discipline*.
23. Garrett Hardin, "The Tragedy of the Commons," *Science, New Series* (162)3859 (1968), 1243–48.
24. Donella H. Meadows, *Thinking in Systems: A Primer*. Edited by Diana Wright (White River Junction, VT: Chelsea Green Publishing, 2015).
25. Senge, *The Fifth Discipline*, 3.
26. Y. Morieux, "Smart Rules: Six Ways to Get People to Solve Problems without You," *Harvard Business Review* (2011).
27. Lee N. Katz, "Lessons from the Marshmallow Challenge." The Turnaround Authority, June 27, 2014. https://theturnaroundauthority.com/2014/06/27/lessons-from-the-marshmallow-challenge/.
28. Leo Bottary and J. Bottary. "Peernovation." Vistage Research Center. Vistage Worldwide, August 26, 2012. https://www.vistage.com/research-center/business-leadership/business-innovation/peernovation/.
29. "A Quote by Phil Jackson." Goodreads. Accessed June 2, 2020. https://www.goodreads.com/quotes/527132-the-strength-of-the-team-is-each-individual-member-the.

30. "A Few Good Men." IMDb.com. Accessed April 26, 2020. https://www.imdb.com/title/tt0104257/characters/nm0000197.
31. "2019 Edelman Trust Barometer." Edelman. Accessed April 27, 2020. https://www.edelman.com/research/2019-edelman-trust-barometer.
32. "Kenneth H. Blanchard Quotes (Author of *The One Minute Manager*)." Goodreads. Accessed April 27, 2020. https://www.goodreads.com/author/quotes/4112157.Kenneth_H_Blanchard.
33. "A Quote from *The Five Dysfunctions of a Team*." Goodreads. Accessed June 2, 2020. https://www.goodreads.com/quotes/218850-remember-teamwork-begins-by-building-trust-and-the-only-way.
34. Kalman J. Kaplan, "On the Ambivalence-Indifference Problem in Attitude Theory and Measurement: A Suggested Modification of the Semantic Differential Technique," *Psychological Bulletin* 77, no. 5 (1972): 361–72. https://doi.org/10.1037/h0032590.
35. John Dewey, *Experience and Education: The 60th Anniversary Edition* (West Lafayette, IN: Kappa Delta Pi, 1998).
36. Margaret E. Brooks, Scott Highhouse, Steven S. Russell, and David C. Mohr, "Familiarity, Ambivalence, and Firm Reputation: Is Corporate Fame a Double-Edged Sword?" *Journal of Applied Psychology* 88, no. 5 (2003): 904–14. https://doi.org/10.1037/0021-9010.88.5.904.
37. Craig Weber, *Conversational Capacity: The Secret to Building Successful Teams That Perform When the Pressure Is On* (New York: McGraw-Hill Education, 2013).
38. Peg Streep, "The Trouble with Trust," *Psychology Today* (March 25, 2014), https://www.psychologytoday.com/us/blog/tech-support/201403/the-trouble-trust.
39. "A Quote by Steve Jobs." Goodreads. Accessed June 2, 2020. https://www.goodreads.com/quotes/8863669-great-things-in-business-are-never-done-by-one-person.
40. James C. Collins, *Good to Great* (London: Random House Business, 2001).
41. Senge, *The Fifth Discipline*, 3.
42. "Larry Bird Quotes." BrainyQuote. Xplore. Accessed June 2, 2020. https://www.brainyquote.com/quotes/larry_bird_368193.
43. John Younker, personal communication, March 2015.
44. Anu Partanen, "What Americans Keep Ignoring about Finland's School Success," *The Atlantic* (February 17, 2017). https://www.theatlantic.com/national/archive/2011/12/what-americans-keep-ignoring-about-finlands-school-success/250564/.
45. James M. Kouzes and Barry Z. Posner. *The Leadership Challenge*. SL: Wiley, 2017.

46 "On the Shoulders of Giants," *American Scientist* (June 23, 2017). https://www.americanscientist.org/article/on-the-shoulders-of-giants.

47 Kouzes and Posner, *The Leadership Challenge*.

48 David Logan and John Paul King, *Tribal Leadership* (London: Collins, 2008).

49 "A Quote by Kahlil Gibran." Goodreads. Accessed May 11, 2020. https://www.goodreads.com/quotes/128983-the-teacher-who-is-indeed-wise-does-not-bid-you.

50 A Quote by Andrew Carnegie." Goodreads. Accessed June 2, 2020. https://www.goodreads.com/quotes/251192-teamwork-is-the-ability-to-work-together-toward-a-common.

51 Craig Weber, "What Is Conversational Capacity and Why Does It Matter?" The Weber Consulting Group. March 27, 2020. Accessed May 7, 2020. https://www.weberconsultinggroup.net/what-is-conversational-capacity-and-why-does-it-matter/.

52 Senge, *The Fifth Discipline*, 3.

53 "A Quote by Margaret Carty." Goodreads. Accessed June 2, 2020. https://www.goodreads.com/quotes/369899-the-nice-thing-about-teamwork-is-that-you-always-have.

54 Bennis, Warren. "Followers Who Tell the Truth Indispensable to Top Leaders," *Sun-Sentinel* (October 6, 2018). Accessed May 12, 2020. https://www.sun-sentinel.com/news/fl-xpm-1990-02-18-9001250151-story.html.

55 "Harry S Truman Quotes." BrainyQuote. Accessed May 12, 2020. https://www.brainyquote.com/quotes/harry_s_truman_109615.

56 Etienne Wenger-Trayner and Beverly Wenger-Trayner. "Introduction to Communities of Practice." BE Wenger-Trayner. 2015. Accessed May 12, 2020. https://wenger-trayner.com/introduction-to-communities-of-practice/

57 Tribune News Service. "No One Can Whistle a Symphony. It Takes a Whole Orchestra to Play It.'—H. E. Luccock." Tribuneindia News Service. Accessed June 2, 2020. https://www.tribuneindia.com/news/archive/thought-for-the-day/no-one-can-whistle-a-symphony-it-takes-a-whole-orchestra-to-play-it-—-he-luccock-818532.

REFERENCES

"2019 Edelman Trust Barometer." Edelman. Accessed April 27, 2020. https://www.edelman.com/research/2019-edelman-trust-barometer.

"A Few Good Men." IMDb.com. Accessed April 26, 2020. https://www.imdb.com/title/tt0104257/characters/nm0000197.

"A Quote by Andrew Carnegie." Goodreads. Accessed June 2, 2020. https://www.goodreads.com/quotes/251192-teamwork-is-the-ability-to-work-together-toward-a-common.

"A Quote by Helen Keller." Goodreads. Accessed June 2, 2020. https://www.goodreads.com/quotes/9411-alone-we-can-do-so-little-together-we-can-do.

"A Quote by Kahlil Gibran." Goodreads. Accessed May 11, 2020. https://www.goodreads.com/quotes/128983-the-teacher-who-is-indeed-wise-does-not-bid-you.

"A Quote by Kenneth H. Blanchard." Goodreads. Accessed June 2, 2020. https://www.goodreads.com/quotes/56863-none-of-us-is-as-smart-as-all-of-us.

"A Quote by Margaret Carty." Goodreads. Accessed June 2, 2020. https://www.goodreads.com/quotes/369899-the-nice-thing-about-teamwork-is-that-you-always-have.

"A Quote by Phil Jackson." Goodreads. Accessed June 2, 2020. https://www.goodreads.com/quotes/527132-the-strength-of-the-team-is-each-individual-member-the.

"A Quote by Ryunosuke Satoro." Goodreads. Accessed June 2, 2020. https://www.goodreads.com/quotes/479992-individually-we-are-one-drop-together-we-are-an-ocean.

"A Quote by Steve Jobs." Goodreads. Accessed June 2, 2020. https://www.goodreads.com/quotes/8863669-great-things-in-business-are-never-done-by-one-person.

"A Quote from *The Five Dysfunctions of a Team*." Goodreads. Accessed June 2, 2020. https://www.goodreads.com/quotes/218850-remember-teamwork-begins-by-building-trust-and-the-only-way.

Apollo 13 Mission Report. Houston, September 1970. https://www.hq.nasa.gov/alsj/a13/A13_MissionReport.pdf

"*Apollo 13* Quotes." Movie Quotes.com. Accessed April 26, 2020. https://www.moviequotes.com/s-movie/apollo-13/.

"Artificial Intelligence." Oxford Reference. Accessed April 26, 2020. https://www.oxfordreference.com/view/10.1093/oi/authority.20110803095426960.

Bennis, Warren. "Followers Who Tell the Truth Indispensable to Top Leaders." *Sun-Sentinel*. October 06, 2018. Accessed May 12, 2020. https://www.sun-sentinel.com/news/fl-xpm-1990-02-18-9001250151-story.html

Bersin, Josh. "The Power of Collaborative Learning: More Important Than Ever." May 20, 2019. https://joshbersin.com/2019/05/the-power-of-collaborative-learning-more-important-than-ever/.

Bottary, Leo. "An Open Letter to Cable News." Vistage Research Center. Vistage Worldwide, May 5, 2011. https://www.vistage.com/

research-center/business-leadership/strategic-communications/an-open-letter-to-cable-n/.

Bottary, Leo. *What Anyone Can Do: How Surrounding Yourself with the Right People Will Drive Change, Opportunity, and Personal Growth*. New York: Bibliomotion, Inc., 2019.

Bottary, Leo, and J. Bottary. "Peernovation." Vistage Research Center. Vistage Worldwide, August 26, 2012. https://www.vistage.com/research-center/business-leadership/business-innovation/peernovation/.

Braun, William. "The System Archetypes." February 27, 2002.

"Briefing Paper One: Systems Thinking." Systems Thinking. Accessed April 26, 2020. http://www.reallylearning.com/Free_Resources/Systems_Thinking/systems_thinking.html.

Brooks, Margaret E., Scott Highhouse, Steven S. Russell, and David C. Mohr. "Familiarity, Ambivalence, and Firm Reputation: Is Corporate Fame a Double-Edged Sword?" *Journal of Applied Psychology* 88, no. 5 (2003): 904–14. https://doi.org/10.1037/0021-9010.88.5.904.

Checkland, Peter. "Systems Theory and Management Thinking." *Critical Issues in Systems Theory and Practice*, 1995, 1–14. https://doi.org/10.1007/978-1-4757-9883-8_1.

Collins, James C. *Good to Great*. London: Random House Business, 2001.

Dewey, John. *Experience and Education: The 60th Anniversary Edition*. West Lafayette, IN: Kappa Delta Pi, 1998.

"Digital Media Literacy: What Is an Echo Chamber?" GCFGlobal.org. Accessed April 26, 2020. https://edu.gcfglobal.org/en/digital-media-literacy/what-is-an-echo-chamber/1/.

Editor, *Business News Daily*. "Business Advice from Albert Einstein: Business Tips." *Business News Daily*. businessnewsdaily.com, April

19, 2012. https://www.businessnewsdaily.com/2381-albert-einstein-business-tips.html.

Goodman, Michael. "Systems Thinking: What, Why, When, Where, and How?" The Systems Thinker, August 16, 2016. https://thesystemsthinker.com/systems-thinking-what-why-when-where-and-how/.

"Harry S Truman Quotes." BrainyQuote. Accessed May 12, 2020. https://www.brainyquote.com/quotes/harry_s_truman_109615.

How Wolves Change Rivers. Sustainable Human. February 13, 2014. Accessed May 08, 2020. https://www.youtube.com/watch?v=ysa5OBhXz-Q.

Kaplan, Kalman J. "On the Ambivalence-Indifference Problem in Attitude Theory and Measurement: A Suggested Modification of the Semantic Differential Technique." *Psychological Bulletin* 77, no. 5 (1972): 361–72. https://doi.org/10.1037/h0032590.

Katz, Lee N. "Lessons from the Marshmallow Challenge." The Turnaround Authority, June 27, 2014. https://theturnaroundauthority.com/2014/06/27/lessons-from-the-marshmallow-challenge/.

"Kenneth H. Blanchard Quotes (Author of *The One Minute Manager*)." Goodreads. Accessed April 27, 2020. https://www.goodreads.com/author/quotes/4112157.Kenneth_H_Blanchard.

Kouzes, James M., and Barry Z. Posner. *The Leadership Challenge*. SL: Wiley, 2017.

"Larry Bird Quotes." BrainyQuote. Xplore. Accessed June 2, 2020. https://www.brainyquote.com/quotes/larry_bird_368193.

Logan, David, and John Paul King. *Tribal Leadership*. London: Collins, 2008.

Meadows, Donella H. *Thinking in Systems: A Primer*. Edited by Diana Wright. White River Junction, VT: Chelsea Green Publishing, 2015.

Morieux, Y. "Smart Rules: Six Ways to Get People to Solve Problems without You." *Harvard Business Review*, 2011.

"On the Shoulders of Giants." *American Scientist*, June 23, 2017. https://www.americanscientist.org/article/on-the-shoulders-of-giants.

Partanen, Anu. "What Americans Keep Ignoring about Finland's School Success." *The Atlantic*. February 17, 2017. https://www.theatlantic.com/national/archive/2011/12/what-americans-keep-ignoring-about-finlands-school-success/250564/.

Shapiro, Leon, and Leo Bottary. *The Power of Peers: How the Company You Keep Drives Leadership, Growth, & Success*. Brookline, MA: Bibliomotion, 2016.

Stanford University. "Text of Steve Jobs's Commencement Address (2005)." *Stanford News*, June 12, 2017. https://news.stanford.edu/2005/06/14/jobs-061505/.

Streep, Peg. "The Trouble with Trust." *Psychology Today*. March 25, 2014. https://www.psychologytoday.com/us/blog/tech-support/201403/the-trouble-trust.

Weber, Craig. *Conversational Capacity: The Secret to Building Successful Teams That Perform When the Pressure Is On*. New York: McGraw-Hill Education, 2013.

Weber, Craig. "What Is Conversational Capacity and Why Does It Matter?" The Weber Consulting Group. March 27, 2020. Accessed May 07, 2020. https://www.weberconsultinggroup.net/what-is-conversational-capacity-and-why-does-it-matter/.

Wenger-Trayner, Etienne, and Beverly Wenger-Trayner. "Introduction to Communities of Practice." BE Wenger-Trayner. 2015. Accessed May 12, 2020. https://wenger-trayner.com/introduction-to-communities-of-practice/.

www.ingramcontent.com/pod-product-compliance
Lightning Source LLC
Chambersburg PA
CBHW032023170526
45157CB00002B/837